DZOGCHEN TEACHINGS

DZOGCHEN TEACHINGS

Chögyal Namkhai Norbu

Edited by
Jim Valby and Adriano Clemente

Snow Lion Publications
Ithaca, New York • Boulder Colorado

Snow Lion Publications
P. O. Box 6483
Ithaca, NY 14851 USA
(607) 273-8519
www.snowlionpub.com

IPC – 434EN06 – Approved by the International Publications Committee
of the Dzogchen Community founded by Chögyal Namkhai Norbu.

Printed in Canada on acid-free recycled paper.

ISBN-10 1-55939-243-6
ISBN-13 978-1-55939-243-3

Library of Congress Cataloging-in-Publication Data

Namkhai Norbu, 1938-
  Dzogchen teachings / Chogyal Namkhai Norbu ; edited by Jim Valby
and Adriano Clemente.
    p. cm.
  ISBN-13: 978-1-55939-243-3 (alk. paper)
  ISBN-10: 1-55939-243-6 (alk. paper)
  1. Rdzogs-chen. I. Valby, Jim, 1946-   . II. Clemente, Adriano. III. Title.
BQ7662.4.N3356 2006
294.3'420423—dc22

                                                    2006007689

DZOGCHEN TEACHINGS

Chögyal Namkhai Norbu

Edited by
Jim Valby and Adriano Clemente

Snow Lion Publications
Ithaca, New York • Boulder Colorado

Snow Lion Publications
P. O. Box 6483
Ithaca, NY 14851 USA
(607) 273-8519
www.snowlionpub.com

IPC – 434EN06 – Approved by the International Publications Committee
of the Dzogchen Community founded by Chögyal Namkhai Norbu.

Printed in Canada on acid-free recycled paper.

ISBN-10 1-55939-243-6
ISBN-13 978-1-55939-243-3

Library of Congress Cataloging-in-Publication Data

Namkhai Norbu, 1938-
   Dzogchen teachings / Chogyal Namkhai Norbu ; edited by Jim Valby
and Adriano Clemente.
      p. cm.
   ISBN-13: 978-1-55939-243-3 (alk. paper)
   ISBN-10: 1-55939-243-6 (alk. paper)
   1. Rdzogs-chen. I. Valby, Jim, 1946-   . II. Clemente, Adriano. III. Title.
   BQ7662.4.N3356 2006
   294.3'420423—dc22
                                                      2006007689

Contents

Preface

Chögyal Namkhai Norbu's *Dzogchen Teachings* is a collection of newly edited oral teachings originally published in the *Mirror*, the newspaper of the international Dzogchen Community established in Italy in 1991 by Chögyal Namkhai Norbu Rinpoche. Dzogchen Master Chögyal Namkhai Norbu was born in 1938 in east Tibet, and began teaching in the West in 1976. After having been invited to Rome, Italy in 1959 by the Tibetologist Professor Giuseppe Tucci, Chögyal Namkhai Norbu became Professor of Oriental Studies at the University of Naples. He continued in that position from 1964 to 1993.

For the last twenty-five years, Rinpoche has worked to establish communities of practitioners throughout the world, and has given numerous public talks as well as over three hundred retreats. This book is a rich collection of precious teachings given by Rinpoche to his students in order to benefit their understanding of the Dzogchen tradition and its value in the modern world.

Dzogchen is the essence of Tibetan Buddhism. Although Dzogchen, or the path of Total Perfection, is not a religion, tradition, or philosophy, it is, as Chögyal Namkhai Norbu says, "the path of self-liberation that enables one to discover one's true nature. It is not only the name of a teaching, but the reality of our true condition, our own totally self-perfected state. Through the transmission, the teacher gives you methods for discovering that true condition."

Through his clear, direct, and precise explanations and instructions, Master Chögyal Namkhai Norbu makes these profound teachings in the lineage of Garab Dorje accessible to everyone. *Dzogchen Teachings* offers an extensive and broad compilation of teachings by a great Dzogchen master and Tibetan scholar. All the chapters contain beneficial instruction for both beginning and advanced students regardless of which tradition they may follow, and insights into the genuine meaning of important subjects related to Sutra, Tantra, and Dzogchen.

This book has been organized according to various topics related to all aspects of Buddhism and Dzogchen, and although there may be redundancies, the editors felt it was important not to remove anything, as the context in which they occur is always different. Some statements suitable for a live teaching situation were removed to maintain literary cohesiveness.

We are pleased to present the vast wisdom and breadth of knowledge found within these pages, and it is the intention of the editors that the publishing of these teachings to the worldwide community will benefit those interested in the study and practice of Dzogchen. We would also like to extend our gratitude to Jim Valby for the final editing of the original versions, and to Adriano Clemente for ordering the chapters and writing the footnotes. We also wish to thank Igor Legati for coordinating the project, and Steven Landsberg for revising the final draft.

Naomi Zeitz
Managing Editor, *The Mirror*
www.melong.com

1   Discovering Our Real Nature[1]

When we follow a teaching, the main point is that we understand what the teaching really is, and its purpose. There is something concrete in the teaching for daily life. What is the use of receiving these teachings if they are not understood, and we only seek techniques of practice? Techniques are useful for understanding and as methods for realization, but if we go too much after titles, then we have lost the main point. There are hundreds and thousands of titles and techniques, but they are all used for the purpose of discovering our real condition. This is the essential teaching of Buddha, Garab Dorje,[2] and all the important masters.

For example, there are collections of the teachings of Buddha called the *Kangyur* and the *Tengyur*.[3] There are hundreds of volumes. We know that if we are going to study only one sutra or tantra, we need our whole life to really understand its contents and different teachings. In order to learn all these books, we would need many lives. When would we get time to realize? This is our concrete condition. It is relative, and not really the main point. The main point is what Buddha once said: "I discovered something profound and luminous beyond all concepts. I tried to communicate it with words, but nobody understands. So now I will meditate alone in the forest." This verse of Buddha is the conclusion of the teaching.

The teaching is not a title or book. The teaching is not Sutra or Tantra or Dzogchen. The teaching is knowledge and understanding for discovering our real nature. That is all it is; however, it is not easy. That is why the Buddha explained many kinds of teachings according to different circumstances and the various capacities of beings. Some people understand and discover what is communicated and how it should work. However, many people don't understand, do not have that capacity, and must work in a different way. We must explain in various ways. That is why there are many kinds of teachings and techniques.

Some people consider that the teaching means not doing anything, just relaxing, and doing what one feels. That is not the teaching. That is the continuation of samsara. We are always doing that, but no one has realized in this way. Some people think that the teaching is judging, analyzing, thinking, and then establishing a point of view; but this is not the sense of the teaching, because everything is relative.

DIRECT INTRODUCTION

As there are three ways of communicating related to our three aspects of existence—the physical body, energy, and mind—similarly, the teaching is communicated by working on these three levels, which are characteristic of the teaching. For introducing knowledge in Dzogchen we use direct introduction. This doesn't mean we are going to a teacher or a powerful realized being, and we stand in front of that teacher and get awakened or realized after spending a little time with him or her.

Many people have this idea, but this is not direct introduction. Nobody can do that—not even Buddha Shakyamuni. If Buddha Shakyamuni could do that, why didn't he do that for all sentient beings instantly? Why isn't everybody realized? Buddha has infinite compassion. He is not missing any amount of compassion for doing actions for others. Buddha is omniscient; he knows the condition of samsara and suffering, so there would be no reason for him not to do that. But that is not the way it happens.

Even if there is a fantastic teacher, a realized being, and we receive a little vibration from that master, we still can't realize our nature in this way. If we go to a teacher, the teacher teaches; that is why he or she is called a teacher. The teacher teaches and does not only sit or meditate. The teacher teaches us how to get in our real nature—explaining with words and ordinary language. That is called oral transmission. That's the reason why a teacher gives retreats and teachings and explains different methods and ways of discovering our real nature for hours and hours. It's not because the teacher likes to talk. If the teacher did not talk, how could people understand what the direct transmission means?

The teacher gives examples, and explains using symbols like the mirror, the crystal, and a peacock's feather. Using these symbols, we can understand our real condition and potentiality. With these symbols and explanations we can have an idea. Once this has been explained, you are more or less ready to receive direct transmission. In this case, the teacher gives you instructions of what you must do in order to have direct experience. It could be that you are doing it together with the teacher, or that you receive the instructions, apply them, and discover. That is called direct introduction. It's important that you understand this.

Sometimes people read Dzogchen books and teachings in which direct transmission is explained—what Garab Dorje said about it, and the method of entering our real nature. Some people have the idea that the teacher can give direct introduction like a gift or an object. They go to the teacher and ask, "Please give me direct introduction." And they think, "Oh, maybe the teacher is not giving direct introduction to everyone, so if I ask the teacher alone, then he or she will give it only to me." This is not true. If teachers could give realization to all sentient beings, then they always would. The teacher likes it if all sentient beings are realizing and getting in their real nature, but this is not always easy.

For that reason we need to work and explain one by one, orally and with symbols, constructing very precise ideas. Then we can go into the instruction of direct transmission. In this way we can have knowledge and understanding, and can really have a sense of the teaching. We must remember that this is the principle. At a retreat lasting many days we learn various techniques; however, we must remember that the purpose of all of them is that principle, to discover our real nature, particularly if we are following the Dzogchen teaching.

2 The Real Condition of All Phenomena[4]

When we speak of Dharma teachings, there are many different forms and traditions, but the principle is neither the form nor the tradition. Dharma means "knowledge, understanding." The term *dharma* comes from Sanskrit, and the real meaning is "all phenomena." That means we need to have knowledge and understanding of all phenomena.

In general, people say, "We are following Dharma," and speak of it as a kind of religion created by Buddha Shakyamuni. That is not a correct point of view. Buddha never created any kind of school or religion. Buddha was a totally enlightened being, someone beyond our limited point of view. The teaching of the Buddha is to have presence in that knowledge.

If we are interested in Dharma, we are interested in knowledge and in understanding the real condition of all phenomena. How can we gain such knowledge? It does not mean we learn in an intellectual way, merely in the condition of subject and object, judging and considering things outside us.

Generally we have the idea, "I am here. I see these objects in front of me and I consider that this is good, that is bad." In this way we perform many types of analysis through which we develop infinite limitations. For that reason the Buddha taught from the beginning that we should not only look outwards, but should observe ourselves a little. Working in that way, we can discover what the real situation is.

When we speak of the Buddha's teaching, we speak of three different *yanas,* or vehicles,[5] the roots of which are all in the teachings he gave in his lifetime in India. We can also study how Buddha transmitted this teaching.

SUFFERING

There is a teaching that is universal to all Buddhists called the Four Noble Truths.[6] This was the first teaching transmitted by Buddha. Even if we have different methods in the teaching, such as Tantra and Dzogchen, they are always based on the Four Noble Truths. Why are they called the Noble Truths? They are noble because they are important for knowledge and understanding.

For example, in the Four Noble Truths, we start with the understanding of suffering. In general, suffering is not so difficult to understand. Even if we know what it is, we are distracted and not present, and, in particular, we are not aware that suffering has a cause. Suffering is the fruit, or the effect of a cause. If there is an effect or a fruit, there is a cause. Why did Buddha explain suffering in the first of all his teachings? It is not because it was particularly interesting, or that people wanted to know about it, but because suffering is universal, and everyone has had that experience. Suffering is not a subject about which we can agree or disagree.

If Buddha had explained the nature of mind, for example, there would have been many who agreed or disagreed with him. We human beings are in general very limited. We have very strong egos, and, generally, people are convinced they have knowledge and understanding with their points of view.

First of all, there are many arguments regarding the nature of mind. The main point of Buddha's teaching was not to convince or to argue, but to make clear our real condition. Ordinary people can understand something of which they have concrete experience. If we have no experience, it is difficult to understand or accept anything.

A baby or small child, for example, has no experience of life. They do not know their condition or their limitations. When we tell children not to touch the fire, we say, "You'll hurt yourself." If the child has no experience of fire, it is very difficult for the child to accept; but if the child touches the fire, then the child will have direct experience. When they see the fire burning, they will not touch it again. Of course this is an experience of suffering—a concrete problem that everyone has—but we do not think much about the cause.

KARMA

When we have problems, we start to struggle with these problems directly. We say, "Where there is a problem, there is also a solution through struggling." Buddha first explained that the condition of suffering is something unpleasant, and nobody likes it. If you do not want suffering, you must research into the cause of suffering. To overcome the problem, the solution is not to struggle or fight.

In order to discover the cause, there are explanations of causes and effects and the relationship between them. All Buddhists and Hindus speak of karma. For most people in Asia, karma is familiar; however, it is not so familiar in the Western world. Although some people find the concept hard to accept and they do not use the word, they accept karma because there is always a cause, an effect, and a relationship with time. Everyone accepts this. That is the main point.

Buddha explained in the Sutra teaching, using hundreds and hundreds of different examples, what cause and effect are, and how they manifest. This teaching is for deepening this knowledge; it is not for just developing the habit to say, "We are Buddhists; we believe that."

I think that karma is very real to everybody, and that it is very important to understand it in the correct way. Some people think of karma as something preprogrammed that we are destined to follow. If problems arise they say, "This is my karma. What can I do?" They are resigned and complacent. This is not a correct understanding of karma. Karma is relative to time and to actual situations in which karma is manifesting.

There is a very famous saying of Buddha Shakyamuni: "To know what we did in our past lives we must examine our present situation." That means we are now human beings; we have a human body, speech, and mind. Our present existence is produced by past karma. Buddha then said, "To know how our next life will be, we must examine our present actions." This means that our present actions can produce the fruit of our next life, and that we can also modify and purify them. We can do anything.

All Buddhist traditions have many different practices for purifying negative karma. This means that when we have the problem of some negative karma, there is also a chance to purify it. We cannot simply say, "This is my karma; there is nothing to do." The potentiality of karma manifests in the way seeds planted in a field grow. They have the potential to produce flowers and something concrete. For example, if we plant a flower seed, a flower grows, not rice or grain. This is called potentiality. In order for the flower to manifest, we need many secondary causes. Even though the seed has the potential to produce a flower, it needs to be planted in the earth, receive water, sunshine, and other secondary causes to manifest.

In general, we live in our circumstances, our relative condition, which is like the earth, the water, and the light necessary for a seed to manifest. If we modify our secondary causes, we can change or block negative situations. This is the correct way to consider karma and its manifestation, and is also the reason why we do purification practice.

CESSATION

How can we stop the cause of negative karma? If we do not want to suffer, then first we must understand that suffering is produced by a cause. When we have discovered the cause, we must stop it. If we do not stop the cause, even if we have knowledge of cause and effect, this understanding does not benefit us. Therefore, after explaining cause and effect, Buddha taught the Third Noble Truth of Cessation.

For example, illness can be produced by food, our attitude, or our way of living. There is always a cause that produces disease. Somehow we must discover what the cause is. If we cannot discover the cause on our own, then we visit a doctor because they are experts. After examining and diagnosing us, the doctor will discover the cause and effect. Somehow we are following a teaching and a teacher, and we learn what the cause of suffering is. When we discover through the teaching and the teacher what the real situation is, then we also receive the solution for stopping it. For example, the doctor advises us not to eat or drink certain foods and beverages, and to change our attitude. Usually the doctor also gives us some medicine. In order to benefit, we must apply this prescription. This is how we can stop the cause of negativities.

EMOTIONS

In the teachings, one of the Buddha's names is "Great Physician." This does not mean that the Buddha prepares certain herbal medicines or analyzes illnesses. All of our illnesses and problems are rooted in our emotions. Ordinarily, we are totally conditioned by our emotions, and are not even aware of how conditioned we are. This is our illness.

If we do not know how to overcome the root of our problems, it is not easy to overcome such things as physical ailments. For example, in Tibetan or Ayurvedic medicine, the three humors—wind, bile, and phlegm—are always explained. These characteristic conditions govern our existence as body, speech, and mind. If our humors are balanced, we will not have many physical problems; but when these three are out of balance, we can have problems. The three humors are rooted in three principal emotions—ignorance or lack of clarity, anger, and attachment. We are conditioned by these, and they are also the cause of all problems. If we do not want to have the effects of suffering, then we must stop these causes. That is what the Buddha explained in the Third Noble Truth.

THE PATH

In order to bring to an end to various causes, there are many different solutions that depend mainly on the condition of the individual. Some people have more capacity and opportunity, and some people less. Buddha is omniscient, which means he has total knowledge and understanding of the situation of samsara. For that reason, in order to transmit knowledge and understanding, Buddha works for each person accordingly, one after another, like a good physician.

If a good doctor is diagnosing and treating people's illnesses, he or she must do it individually, to see what the situation of each person is. Sometimes we can prepare a kind of universal medicine that benefits everybody; but if you want to cure someone in a perfect way, then you must go into the situation of the individual and see what his or her actual condition is. For that reason, the Fourth Noble Truth is called the Noble Truth of the Path.

Buddha taught different kinds of paths. This does not mean that Buddha created different kinds of schools, but that he transmitted knowledge and understanding in various ways, according to the condition of the individual. Thus, we have the different teachings of Sutra, Tantra, and Dzogchen—teachings particularly related to the condition of the three existences of the individual.

Firstly, we have our physical body, which is relative to our physical world on the material level. Accordingly, the Buddha manifested physically, and taught and transmitted the Sutra teaching.

Tantra

In general, Tantra is a Sanskrit word used also in Hinduism; but even though the same word is used, it does not always have the same meaning. In the Tantric teachings of the Buddhist tradition, *tantra* means our real condition. In the real sense, *tantra* means "continuity," or "continuation." What does continuity of our real nature mean? It means a recognition or understanding of our energy level.

For example, we have infinite thoughts arising that can be good or bad. We also have a conception of good and bad, but the root of these thoughts is relative to our energy, a kind of movement of thought, the source of which is part of our real condition. If we observe a thought, where is it? Where does it go? When we observe it, we cannot find anything. What we always find is emptiness, the real condition of all things, the *Dharmadhatu*.

Immediately after one thought, another thought arises. When we observe this second thought, it disappears, and we find only emptiness. Immediately after that, the third and fourth thoughts arise, and this continues infinitely. We have this infinite movement because we have that potentiality, that energy, in our nature. This is the real meaning of continuation—continuation of emptiness and movement, energy and movement, again and again, without interruption. That knowledge and understanding is the principle of the Tantric teaching, and is related more to our energy level.

Although not transmitted on the physical level by the Buddha, this teaching was transmitted through his manifestation. This is a characteristic feature of Tantric teaching. Those who follow this kind of teaching need more capacity to follow and understand. The physical level is always easier to understand. For example, if you see someone coming, what you see is their physical body. It is not so easy to see the energy level of that person. If someone had no physical body, but was only energy or mind, you wouldn't be able to see them. If you could, it would mean you had a special capacity. That is an example of how energy is more difficult to understand.

DZOGCHEN

Dzogchen, a Tibetan word, is *Santi Maha* in the language of Oddiyana,[7] or *Maha Santi* in Sanskrit, and refers to a perfected state, the potentiality and power of our real nature. We can discover that knowledge, that potentiality, that real condition. This is a teaching related more to the mind. In order to understand the Dzogchen teaching, we need capacity on that mind level. Of course, if we want to know or discover something at that level, it is more difficult than at the physical level.

In any case, there are, mainly, three characteristic teachings relative to the three aspects of an individual's existence. Sometimes it is important to know the characteristics of the teachings. It does not mean that we are comparing them, and saying, "This teaching is better than that one." It simply depends on the situation and capacity of the individual. If there were no differences among individuals, there would be no reason to have different kinds of paths. If there are different paths, there are different reasons for them. The main point of the teaching in general is to understand our condition concretely. That is the purpose of Dharma. Knowledge of Dharma is knowledge of the understanding of all the phenomena we can have when we discover our real condition.

The way in which the Buddhist teaching developed in the world in different places is relative to the culture and knowledge of the country. Trisong Deutsen (742-797) was a famous Dharma king who was responsible for the diffusion of Buddhism in Tibet in the eighth century. He invited the very famous Indian pandit Shantarakshita to teach the Buddhist sutras, but he had many problems spreading the Buddhist teachings. This is because in Tibet, before the introduction of Buddhism, there was an ancient tradition called Bön,[8] a tradition which was completely different from Buddhism, and which was considered by some Western scholars to be one of the roots of shamanism. This ancient tradition focuses upon the concept of energy. Their followers studied and developed the knowledge of energy, and its relation to the individual and the external world.

For an individual who is interested in the Dharma, the most essential point is to discover our real condition. If we discover how our real condition is, then we can discover the condition of others. If we do not discover ourselves, and we judge and consider things outside us, it is impossible to discover the condition of all phenomena. That is why in all the Buddha's teachings—Sutra, Tantra, and Dzogchen—it is said that one should observe oneself. We cannot control the universe outside, but we can control ourselves. If there is some evolution within ourselves, this may also be useful for others.

3 The Difference between Sutra and Tantra [9]

In the Sutra teachings, the term *Dharma* is frequently used, and the fundamental meaning of Dharma refers to our own real condition as the Dharmakaya. The term *tantra* also refers to our real condition; however, there is a difference in the views of Sutra and Tantra regarding the nature of our real condition, and it is important to know and understand that.

In the Sutra teachings we speak mainly of *shunyata*—the emptiness or absence of self-existence or self-nature of all phenomena. When you are explaining the Sutra teachings, you must always explain *shunyata* and compassion. What is referred to by the term *shunyata* is absolute truth, or the absolute condition. Then there is also relative truth, and two different ways of experiencing the relative condition, depending on whether you have real knowledge and understanding or not.

If, for example, you have the realization of the Bodhisattva level, you still, of course, have impure vision, but you are not conditioned by it; and you have the awareness that everything is unreal, like a dream. In that case, even if you still have ordinary vision, your vision is different from that of an ordinary person. We consider compassion to be part of the relative level, because if we know that there are many sentient beings who have no real knowledge of Dharma, Dharmakaya, or absolute truth, and we ourselves have such knowledge, we will automatically feel compassion for those who do not.

For those who do not have real knowledge—even if it is ultimately true that there is no "I" or "we," and even if it is true that the dualistic perception they experience is an illusion—they are nevertheless conditioned by it. To be distracted and conditioned in this way is what it means to be caught in samsara, and there is infinite suffering in that condition or state. This is why compassion is essential at the relative level. The Sutra practitioner has that knowledge or understanding, and tries to develop compassion and bodhichitta on the relative level as much as possible, while at the same time trying to get into the Dharmakaya, or absolute, state. This is how you apply the Sutra teachings.

In the Sutra teachings, absolute truth, or *nirvana*, is considered to be the absolute or real condition. What is this absolute truth? It is the knowledge of *shunyata*, total emptiness. But total emptiness does not mean that no relative condition exists—on the relative level, everything manifests as the world we experience, even if our actual nature is emptiness. We are distracted by this, and therefore experience samsara and suffering.

In the Sutra teachings, relative truth is called *samsara*. When we speak, for example, of the method of Sutra as being the path of renunciation, what is it that we are renouncing? We are renouncing the relative condition, and trying to find ourselves in the absolute condition. This is what is meant by *samsara* and *nirvana*—nirvana being the experience of true knowledge of the real nature of phenomena, which is emptiness, or the Dharmakaya state. This is the point of view found in the Sutra teachings.

In the Tantric teachings, there is more knowledge of the energy level, which is not found in the Sutra system. We can say that this point is not addressed in the Sutra system because the Sutra teachings are for those who have no capacity for that knowledge. If you have that knowledge, that capacity, then you apply Tantra. This is why there are Tantric teachings.

Many people are more accustomed to doing practice in the Sutra style, and when they speak of meditation, for example, they always consider it to be sitting with crossed legs and closed eyes. In the Sutra teachings, there are gradual and nongradual methods. The origins of the latter methods are to be found in the history of all the present-day schools of Zen.

Zen methods are nowadays very developed; and since many methods from different sources have been integrated with them, they no longer exist exactly as they did in ancient times. Nevertheless, even if they have been altered over time, they are still based on the Sutra teachings. This is why, in Zen, it is believed that the main point of practice is to get into the state of *shunyata*, or voidness, and to remain in it. That is what meditation is considered to be in Zen.

In any kind of Sutra teaching, meditation involves sitting silently in a quiet place. Many people are attached to that form of practice, and some people have an aversion to Tantrism because they feel that it requires too many things to recite and construct, and the use of many ritual instruments for doing rites and pujas and so on. Such people prefer to simply meditate in silence.

CONTEMPLATION

It is true that meditating or contemplating is the main path to realization, and, of course, everybody acknowledges that. Tantric practitioners also like meditating and applying contemplation, but we must understand what we really mean by meditation. Meditation doesn't only mean sitting somewhere with closed eyes. That is just one way to do meditation. Meditation means working with the experience of emptiness. If through this experience you develop knowledge of contemplation, your practice may really become true contemplation; but if it does not, you just remain in that state of emptiness, or *shunyata*.

The state of emptiness is just an experience, and there are many kinds of meditation experiences that are not contemplation. Some people say that between two thoughts there is an empty space, and that is the state of contemplation. They believe that contemplation just means extending this empty space between thoughts. Some people write and think this way, and consider that to be the teaching of the Buddha; however, that is not the teaching of the Buddha at all. Being in the state of emptiness means that we are simply having a particular experience. Thinking that everything is empty, and being in that state, is only an experience of emptiness, but it is still very far from being in the state of contemplation.

Real contemplation means being in our real condition, which includes not only emptiness, but also movement. If we have no capacity for integrating or being in that movement, we are very far from our real condition.

MOVEMENT

Tantric teachings have more understanding of movement, and they consider movement to be a part of our real nature. There are many aspects to this movement, including the level of the physical body, the aspect of energy related to voice, and the level of mind. If you visualize, for example, that this house is not an ordinary house, but a mandala, a pure dimension of lights and forms, and you transform this house and dimension into a mandala, what are you doing? You are working with your mind; you are thinking. That process of thinking is not a static contemplation; it involves the movement of your mind.

If you are present in that movement, that is contemplation. You can be in a state of contemplation while experiencing movement. If you have an experience of emptiness, that is not yet contemplation; however, if you are in the state of instant presence in that emptiness, at that moment, you are in the state of contemplation. What is the difference between being in emptiness or in movement? There is no difference.

The same is also true for physical movement, which is why in Tantra there are many methods, such as Yantra Yoga movements and sacred dances. Of course, it depends on who is dancing. If you have real knowledge of the Tantric teachings, you know how to move, and, at the same time, be in the state of contemplation. Then, if you dance all day, or sit all day without moving, there is no difference. The Tantric teachings make more use of movement than Sutra, because someone with the capacity to integrate with movement can perhaps become realized more quickly. Movement also exists at the level of our energy, so in Tantra the method of transformation involves integrating everything into that principle. I am not saying that it is easy to integrate and enter into that knowledge—it takes a long time and it is not easy at all—but it is very important that you know how Tantric methods work, and understand what contemplation means.

If you do transformation practice visualizing a mandala, and are only working with your mind, thinking for hours and hours and developing transformation in that way without knowing its final goal, which is to be in that clarity while in the state of instant presence—if you miss this principle, then there is not much purpose or meaning. It is the same as living in an empty state for days and days, and having no knowledge of how to be in real, instant presence in that state.

VAJRA

The symbol of Tantra is the vajra, which has five points at both ends and a sphere in the middle. That sphere, or *thigle*, represents our potentiality, which means that our real condition is beyond limitations and any kind of division into this aspect or that. At the relative level, there are manifestations of all kinds of aspects, and the two main aspects are impure and pure vision, which we normally call *samsara* and *nirvana*. In the Sutra teachings they are referred to as "relative" and "absolute" truth respectively, while in Tantra, "impure vision" corresponds to the five aggregates, and "pure vision" to the five Sambhogakaya Buddhas.[10] In the symbol of the vajra, both these aspects are linked to the central sphere, which reminds us that in a real sense both of them are our own nature, our own energy. Energy is part of our real nature.

TRANSFORMATION

Based on this recognition of energy as being part of our own nature, the Tantric teachings work with the path of transformation. When we speak of transformation, it means that we understand the true value of things. At the level of samsara, or impure vision, we have the five emotions, but in Tantra we understand that their inherent nature is energy. That energy is our real nature. Only the ways that energy manifests are

28

different. That which manifests as the five passions when we have impure vision manifests as the five wisdoms in pure vision. In the central sphere, or *thigle,* of the vajra, both of its seemingly opposite ends join, showing that pure and impure vision, afflictions and wisdoms, are both aspects of our own energy. At the level of the *thigle,* there is no difference between the two manifestations. That is the knowledge of Tantric teachings.

CONTINUATION

Why is this level of teaching and practice called Tantra? The real meaning of *tantra* is "continuation," or "continuity," something continuing without interruption, which is considered our real nature. But what is it that continues? And how? We can discover this by observing ourselves. For example, if we observe ourselves, we know that we have thoughts. If we observe attentively where the thought is, where it arises from, and where it disappears to, we can search for a long time, but we won't find anything concrete.

What we find in the end is always emptiness, because that is the basis of our condition. When we try to find our thoughts, we find this Base from which thoughts proceed. Even if we find the Base, that doesn't mean that our thoughts disappear forever. After a few seconds we have another thought. We can observe it again, but we won't find anything. We can do this research for many days, but we will find only emptiness. At the same time, we also have countless thoughts that are continually arising. This continuation of thought is also part of our condition, and in this way we can find that our condition is the alternation of thoughts and emptiness. Emptiness is the Base, and thoughts are its manifestation.

This manifestation occurs because there is a continuation of energy. Since this is so, how can we remain in our real nature? If we think a little of how thoughts arise, sometimes it seems that there is a connection between one thought and the next, but in the real sense they are not connected; there is always an empty space between two thoughts. If we are doing practice like Shine[11]—the meditation practice used to develop a calm state—sometimes we can discover that this empty space is experienced for a longer duration, and we can stay for some seconds in it without any thought arising in the mind. We have a longer experience of emptiness, and then we notice that a thought arises again.

Without practice, just observing the ordinary way we habitually think, it is sometimes not so easy to discover this empty space; but in the real sense, thoughts and empty space are always alternating continuously whether we are aware of this or not. That continuity is our real nature, and that is what is meant by Tantra. Tantra means our real condition. When you say the word "Tantra," or speak about it, you already have recognition of your own energy.

The commitment of Tantra, particularly of the Higher Tantra, is to train ourselves to remain in pure vision. If you transform into a deity, whether it be peaceful, wrathful, or joyful—depending on your root emotion[12]—transforming your impure vision in this way into pure vision, you are applying that method. When you use this method according to the Tantric point of view, you are always working with pure vision.

If, for example, you are working with your anger, and in order to transform that passion you visualize yourself as a wrathful manifestation, then, when you make that transformation, you are in pure vision, and are no longer bound up in impure vision. When you are angry with someone in the ordinary dualistic state of mind, you are caught up in

thinking that that person is very bad, and that you don't like him or her; you are angry and charged and develop that emotion. This is impure vision.

The anger that you feel is your own energy, so it is not necessary that you stop it. You can transform your feeling, so that instead of being angry with someone, you transform this anger into a wrathful manifestation. You don't manifest as a wrathful form to fight with that person. You are simply no longer caught up in that impure vision. You are in pure vision, so that even if you were to continue for hours and hours in your feeling of anger, you would have no problems. This is an example of how to use your pure vision. Training in pure vision is the *samaya*, or commitment, of the Tantric teachings.

That is good also for Dzogchen practitioners. For example, if you see your Vajra brothers and sisters[13] as enlightened beings, as if they were your teachers, you will never have problems with them. On the other hand, if you always think they are the ones who are creating difficulties, you will always have problems. Thus, it is very useful to train a little in pure vision according to the Tantric system. This is why we also need this knowledge and understanding.

Of course, the methods of the various levels of the path are different. In Tantra we use transformation methods, whereas in Dzogchen the method used is that of self-liberation. If you understand how Tantric methods work, then, when you learn the method of self-liberation as it is practiced in Dzogchen, you can better understand what the difference is between them.

4   The Meaning of Vajra[14]

You already know that Tantric teachings, or higher teachings, are called Vajrayana, and the teachers transmitting that knowledge are called Vajra Acharya. We use the term *vajra* for everything related to this. In the Dzogchen teaching, we have the Ati Buddha, or Primordial Buddha, called Samantabhadra.[15]

Samantabhadra is also represented by the vajra — in Tibetan, *rangjung dorje* — and in the Dzogchen Upadesha there are rich explanations of this. *Rangjung* means "self-originated"; *dorje* or *vajra* means "the real condition." The real condition is Ati Buddha. Therefore Ati Buddha is not considered a particular being, but the symbol of the primordial state of all sentient beings, which is represented with the symbol of the vajra. Even if we symbolize Samantabhadra, our knowledge of the teaching, or our understanding of its principle with the figure of vajra, when referring to the vajra and the bell, the vajra represents the state. Through this symbol, we can understand our real nature, our potentiality. When we are doing practice, or following the teachings, the knowledge of our real nature is called *vajra*, and our understanding of the three dimensions, Dharmakaya, Sambhogakaya, and Nirmanakaya, are the three vajras.

Body, Voice, and Mind

Relatively, in our ordinary condition, we refer to the three states of body, voice, and mind. Our normal body, for example, is an ordinary body. When we say "the vajra of the body," we are referring to the state or real nature of the body—not to flesh and bone and all these things. All these physical things have come from the nature of the elements. When the physical body dissolves, it can return to the nature of the elements. That nature in our real condition is the five colors. When we do visualize our three vajras using the letters white OM, red AH, and blue HUM, we visualize them inside the dimension of a five-colored *thigle,* because it represents the potentiality of the nature of the five elements as the dimension of our body, voice, and mind.

Why do we use this symbol, or form, of the vajra? In the real sense, in the center, there is a ball that represents our potentiality, our real nature. This is the real sense of the *thigle*; the *thigle* is a sphere without angles, which means beyond all limitations. At the same time, it has full potentiality. This is our real nature.

We also symbolize our three dimensions of Dharmakaya, Sambhogakaya, and Nirmanakaya with the vajra. For example, the Dharmakaya is symbolized by the central ball; the Sambhogakaya is the upper five points; and the Nirmanakaya is the lower five points. These are the three kayas. Why are there five points up and five points down? It depends on how we view the vajra. If we rotate it, we can no longer say "up and down," we can say "left and right."

In general, we view things in this way. When we say "up and down," we can also mean "good and bad," "important and less important." Often, in the West, it is said if you do something bad, you go down, and if you do something good, you go up. Up means paradise, but we don't really know if paradise is up or down. This is just our idea. Also, when we consider the physical body, we consider that the head is something more pure and important than the feet. The symbol is presented this way because we have this idea.

This potentiality is infinite, and is not Samantabhadra, or the Buddha, or some other being. You realize that this ball is you—your real nature and potentiality. This central ball has infinite potentiality that does not always manifest. It manifests when there are secondary causes. For example, in the case of the mirror, when reflections manifest it means there are some objects in front of the mirror. The reflections depend on the objects in front of it; if there are no objects in front of the mirror, the mirror has nothing to reflect.

In the same way, even if we have infinite potentiality in our real nature, if there is no secondary cause, there is nothing to manifest. When there are secondary causes it can manifest in two different ways, depending on our condition and our capacity. There is always some manifestation, whether it is up or down. We can manifest either remaining present in our nature, or falling into dualistic vision. There is the possibility of the manifestation of impure vision, or the Nirmanakaya, as this dimension is related to our karmic potentiality. If we fall into dualistic vision with the concept of subject and object and are fully conditioned by that, we are in samsara.

When we don't fall into dualistic vision, then secondary causes manifest how everything is. For example, the mirror can manifest everything as it is, in all its forms, shapes, and colors. The mirror has no idea of subject or object. It always manifests with the qualities of the mirror, always remaining in the state of the ball, and then, through secondary causes, manifests everything, depending on the dimension. That is called the Sambhogakaya. Those are the five points up. In Tantra, five points up represents pure vision, and five points down, impure vision. Whether the manifestation is pure or impure, the real condition is unchanged.

For example, the mirror never changes. Whether there is a pig or a Buddha manifesting in it, for the mirror it is all the same. When we are trying to be in this contemplation, in this ball, at that moment, we are not conditioned by pure or impure vision. But in the case of our dualistic vision, we have infinite karmic potentialities. When we are not established in the state of the center, then we are distracted, and fall completely into the state of dualistic vision.

WORLD PEACE BY WORKING FROM NUMBER ONE

The teachings are for living in this world—for having fewer problems and fewer tensions. Many people speak now about world peace. What does that mean? How can there be world peace if we don't have peace in ourselves? We are each members of society—society meaning all of us together, not as individuals. Since many individuals together make up society, it means that the individuals must have a kind of evolution. Although we have power and military might, and sometimes there are provisional changes, in the real sense it never changes.

Society is made up of many individuals each having their point of view, their feelings, and their sensations. If we want to develop society so that there is more peace and happiness, each one of us must work with our condition. For example, our society is like numbers. When we count, we must always begin with the number "1." If I think about society, I must start with myself as "number one." We all come from that place. When there is number one, there are also many other numbers.

We must try to understand our problems, our limitations, and so on. If we are free of our limitations, we can have some effect. For example, the first time I came from India, I came with a very small piece of luggage. Then I worked at an institute in Rome, and later at a university. Then I met someone who was a little interested in the teaching. During that period no one knew about Dzogchen teachings. Some people knew a little about Zen. First I began explaining to one or two people. Then more and more people became interested, and the numbers grew. At that time no one knew about Dzogchen teachings in the West, and now many people know about it, because they understand about discovering their real condition, and getting in their real nature. In that case I was number one, and in this way it developed.

When you are number one, there is the possibility to develop not only Dzogchen teachings, but knowledge and understanding. If we want peace in the world, we must develop in this way. If people are working and developing in this way, then I believe there is a possibility of peace. I don't have much faith in only one or two nations meeting in some big city to have a big banquet. It's very important that as practitioners on the path, we realize that these things are very important, and, in the real sense, becoming a practitioner means having responsibility.

VIEW, MEDITATION, AND BEHAVIOR

When we ask, "Why?," there is no end to questioning, and we can't find a reason or a "because" that is a final answer. Therefore it's better that we don't use *why* and *because* too much. It's better to go to the root of *why* and *because* without looking too much outside—judging, thinking, and analyzing. It is better that we observe ourselves instead of having a dualistic view.

Using the example of a mirror, if we look in it, we can see our face; we can understand a little how we look. First we can discover how many limitations we have; we limit everything indeed. We discover our false beliefs and our concrete condition. "Concrete condition" doesn't mean we discover our nature of mind. First we discover our limitations. That is very important. Then we discover what "point of view" means, and we discover how we should be in our real condition.

We can find solutions in the teachings' methods. If we use these methods, we can find what we are searching for. If we use practices, we can discover that they are related to using our experiences. For example, Yoga Tantra is not a teaching in which we use our experiences. We use visualizations of deities, chant mantras, and then, somehow, we receive some wisdom. When we are working with visualizations and deities, we are working with our clarity. When we are being in that clarity, we can find ourselves in a state of contemplation.

In our lifetime it is important that we understand that everything is our experience. There is nothing good or bad that is not connected with experience. We should not be distracted by these experiences. If we are practitioners, we see that good or bad does not matter; it is all experience. We work with and use experience, and try to be in the state of knowledge or understanding. Then everything becomes positive for our practice.

In Dzogchen we say that visions are the ornaments of the primordial state. We can have good and bad visions as well as good and bad sensations. As practitioners, however, we don't need to see it that way, and through using our experiences, everything can become the same taste. In that way we overcome our tensions and problems. These are very simple and essential practices in daily life.

In regard to *chödpa,* or conduct, in the Dzogchen context, it is necessary to understand that *chödpa* is not a teaching about a particular kind of conduct or a set of rules. We don't say you should do this or that; this is related to the path of renunciation. In Dzogchen we need to learn our responsibility—self-responsibility. Someone is not coming to guide you; you guide yourself. You don't need particular vows or rules; you control yourself. Of course, according to circumstances, if there is a rule, you can also respect that dimension. If you don't know how to pay respect, it means you are not aware. Thus it is important to cultivate awareness, and to try to be responsible for ourselves.

EDUCATION OF CHILDREN

If you want to educate your small children while they are growing up, you should try to educate them in a particular way. Until they are around ten years old, children cannot control themselves. Letting them do as they wish is not very good. There must be some way you can control children, and help them. From the beginning you explain what kinds of limitations we have in society. We know that educating by setting limitations is not good, but that it is necessary for the condition and functioning of our society. We don't have a free dimension, and if children are trained as though there is such a dimension, then later in life it becomes very difficult for them. They can't integrate into society. It's not necessary to be overly severe with children, but mainly you have to explain and help them to understand, and surely they will.

But the main point is how you explain—for children, this is essential. For example, if you want to teach a small child not to kill, you explain, "You don't kill animals," because sometimes children enjoy killing insects. If you just tell them, "You must not kill because it's not good," they don't really understand why, and the more often you say "No," the more they feel like killing. For example, if you say, "You must not kill because this small insect may be a mother or father or baby; maybe this insect is coming out to find food for its children who are waiting somewhere, and if you kill her, she can't go back, and they will feel very bad." If you explain it in that way, then it is an experience they can relate to. They have a mother and father, maybe a sister and brother, and they may think, "What if someone killed my mother and she couldn't come back, what would I do?" Or, for example, "If some giant stepped on you and killed you, how would you feel?" They can understand with their experience. Then their sense of responsibility arises. You can explain in this way. After ten years of age, children must really be free, and if you see they are really doing something wrong, you try to explain. You don't try to control. This is important in education.

In regard to ourselves, we also observe and reeducate ourselves, and try to be aware, for example, in our eating and drinking in daily life. If people are not able to control their drinking and they become drunk, in the end their realization is illness, or problems. We need to remember that we eat and drink in order to live. If there is no food, we cannot live. Eating and drinking are only examples of hundreds of possible circumstances. Through practicing awareness in eating and drinking, we can realize a little how we can control ourselves.

In conclusion, if we are Dzogchen practitioners, we must be responsible for ourselves. If we don't have that capacity, we should learn and ultimately realize that. This is very important. We need to act responsibly, with awareness. If we are not aware in all circumstances, then we never become responsible. This is the duty of all practitioners.

5 Dzogchen—The Path of Self-Liberation[16]

The Sutra and Tantra teachings are characterized by methods related to the Path of Renunciation and the Path of Transformation. The characteristic method of the Dzogchen teaching is the Path of Self-Liberation. It is very important that you must understand, however, that Dzogchen is not only the title of a teaching.

In general, people use different titles of teachings, such as the Upadesha Series.[17] You consider it something special, but you don't really discover what Dzogchen is. To know or discover the real sense of the Dzogchen teaching you don't need the title of a book or teaching, or some particular type of study, because when you read or follow a book, you are constructing intellectual knowledge. You will never really discover your state of Dzogchen that way.

You can discover it if you listen well and try to understand the meaning of the teaching, and then use the methods. Method means you work concretely with your experience. That is the only way you can discover the real meaning of Dzogchen. This does not belong to any kind of title or book. You must not be conditioned by books; try to understand what is being communicated. That is the principle of your capacity. If someone does not have the capacity to follow in that way in order to discover their real state, then we say that person has no capacity to follow Dzogchen teaching. This doesn't mean, however, that a person cannot read or analyze books.

Westerners in particular have no problem with reading books and analyzing. Everybody knows how to read and judge. People like to read books before they go to sleep. Usually, next to the place where people sleep, there are many interesting books. This is a way to enjoy books, but you will never discover your real nature that way. That is why we must understand the real meaning of the teaching.

TRANSFORMATION

First of all, you must understand what "self-liberation" means. What is the difference between the Path of Self-Liberation and the Path of Transformation? When we say "transformation," we are proceeding from a concept of pure and impure vision. Our state is presented through the symbol of the vajra, with the two aspects of pure and impure dimensions.

If you do not have that concept to begin with, then how and what do you transform? You are transforming impure vision into pure vision. You are transforming your five aggregates into the five Buddhas, and your five elements into the five Yums, or consorts, of the Buddhas, your five emotions into the five wisdoms. Not only do you have a precise concept of pure and impure vision, but you also consider impure as having no value, as having the aspect of samsara. That is why you are transforming it into pure vision.

SELF-LIBERATION

When we speak about self-liberation, we are not proceeding from this concept of transformation. Self-liberation doesn't mean you are transforming something into something else. There is not even this concept of pure or impure. Of course, this doesn't mean that when you are doing Dzogchen practice your impure vision disappears. But when you are in a state of contemplation, there is no concept of pure or impure. Then you are in a state of self-liberation.

You can learn about the principle of self-liberation using the example of the mirror. In the Dzogchen teaching, we use the symbol of the mirror in order to have knowledge and understanding. How? First of all, with a mirror, you must observe yourself, not just look at objects, judging and thinking that this is good or bad, this is pure or impure. When you have this concept, then you also have dualistic vision.

How can you overcome this? You observe yourself instead of looking at the objects. For example, if you are looking in a mirror, you can see your face, your existence. In this way you can discover, for example, what your face looks like. This means that you are observing yourself, and you can discover your limitations, your condition, and your existence.

In general we don't observe ourselves—particularly when we study in an intellectual way. As long as you have the concept that there is your point of view, then there is also the point of view of others. If you are convinced of your own point of view, then you must negate that of others, which means judging everything, looking at objects, and doing analysis—something very different than observing yourself.

VIEW

All traditions of Sutra and Tantra speak about the point of view, or *tawa,* and every school or tradition has its *tawa.* If you are following the Sakyapa[18] tradition, for example, then you will learn the point of view of the Sakyapas. If you are following the Kagyüdpa tradition, then you will learn the Kagyüdpa point of view. Then you will defend the Kagyüdpa point of view and negate the others. There are many arguments between schools and scholars. If you study the Madhyamika and Prajñaparamita[19] texts, then you must follow one of these methods. First you study and follow one school of thought, and then you study another and make a comparison. In any case, there are many arguments.

Why are there these arguments, and why has it developed this way? The reason is that a point of view, or *tawa,* is developed by looking at an object. You consider that this is good, that is bad, judging as though you were looking at an object. Your senses are pointed at an object, and you do an analysis and form a judgment. In that way, maybe, you can develop some type of intellectual study.

For example, if you want to give a university lecture, then you must be able to do some type of analysis; otherwise people will not consider you to be a scholar. That is not, however, the solution for overcoming samsara or obtaining realization. Discovering your own real nature means that you must observe yourself rather than only observing other objects. That is why, in the Dzogchen teaching, we use the example of looking in the mirror.

Looking in the mirror is only an example, because of course you cannot discover all of your limitations and problems by looking at the mirror. By observing your limitations, your existence, your attitude, and your intention, you can discover many of the sources of your problems. The mirror is a symbol that helps you to understand that you must observe yourself instead of judging others.

POTENTIALITY

Another very important function of the mirror is its use for discovering what is meant by our potentiality. All sentient beings, not only human beings, have infinite potentiality. If we are human beings, we can—unlike animals, for example—observe and discover that we have great potentiality. How can we discover this potentiality and its nature? First of all, we must observe ourselves, and then we can know that we have this potentiality. Then, through the example of the mirror, we can understand what being in our real nature means. Knowing, or being in our real nature, means being beyond judgment and analysis. Then we can learn with the example of the mirror.

DUALISTIC VISION

If there is a mirror in front of you, you look in the mirror and see different kinds of reflections. They may be nice or ugly things, big or small, and they may be different colors and shapes. In the Sutra teaching of the Buddha, it says that everything is based on interdependence. An object in front of the mirror and the mirror's capacity to manifest reflections are interdependent. Through that interdependence, the reflection manifests. That reflection is unreal, but you have a very precise idea that the object is real. You still remain in dualistic vision with your concept that you are here, and what you see is there, in the mirror. Reflections appear in the mirror. They are unreal, but we understand the object to be real. You are looking in the mirror,

47

and even though you have at least an idea of "unreal," that is not real knowledge, and has no function. It is only intellectual knowledge. This is our normal condition.

BEING THE MIRROR

When we say that we have knowledge, or that we have discovered our real nature and we are in this nature, that means that we are "being the mirror." You see, "being the mirror" or "looking in the mirror" are two completely different things. If we "are the mirror," then we have no concept of dualistic vision.

If a reflection manifests in the mirror, why is it manifesting? There are two reasons. One is because the mirror has the capacity to manifest infinite reflections. This is the mirror's quality. If there is an object in front of the mirror, whose capacity it is to reflect, naturally a reflection will appear in the mirror. Furthermore, the mirror has no idea of checking or accepting the object it is reflecting. The mirror doesn't need any program for that. This is what is called its qualification, or infinite potentiality.

In the same way, we have infinite potentiality, but we are ignorant of that. When we are ignorant of our real nature, then we always conceive that "I am here" and "the object is there," "I am looking and seeing an object," and so on. We do not discover that we are like a mirror, and if we never discover this, then of course there is no way that we can function like the mirror. When you discover that you are like the mirror, then there is a possibility that you will be the mirror.

When you are the mirror, then you have no problems with reflections—they can be big, small, nice, ugly, any kind. For you, the reflections are only a manifestation of your quality, which is like that of a mirror. When you have no problems with reflections, then you understand self-liberation. You are not changing or transforming something. You are only being in your real nature.

You remember the idea of "the same flavor" in the Mahamudra[20] teaching and the Dzogchen Semde. You can understand this if you are really being the mirror. Whether there is a nice or ugly reflection, there is no difference for you. When you are in your real nature, there is no change at all. That is the real meaning of self-liberation.

DIRECT INTRODUCTION

When a teacher gives a direct transmission it means that the teacher uses methods so that you can have an experience. With such an experience, you can discover, or have an introduction to, your primordial state— or we can say that you come to understand or discover your state of *rigpa,* or "instant presence." You can use different names, but it does not change it at all.

Practice refers to contemplation, which really means that you have that knowledge, and that you are really being in that knowledge, like the mirror. Then we can say that we are in a state of contemplation. Until you have that experience of knowledge, until you discover that state, you can speak about contemplation, but it is only a name. Contemplation is not only an idea, but something we discover with experience. So that is the famous Dzogchen—the state of *rigpa.* Until we discover that state, Dzogchen is only a word.

DIRECT EXPERIENCE

In the Dzogchen teachings, a teacher explains methods that you can apply for discovering that state. When you say that you are practicing or following Dzogchen teachings, it doesn't mean that you are reciting some prayers or mantras, or doing some visualization. It means that, following a teacher and using methods, you discover that state. When you have discovered that state, then you still need many kinds of methods for realizing it. Discovering the state of your real nature and realizing it are completely different things.

Many people have the idea that when they have had some experience or discovery, they are enlightened; however, this discovery does not mean they are enlightened. The state of enlightenment means you have direct knowledge of what the state of *rigpa* is, and you are not just learning through intellectual study. When you follow a teaching in an intellectual way, you have many ideas at first—thinking, judging, and making analysis. You can follow or reject these ideas; but when you have many problems, you discover that perhaps this is not real knowledge. It is like following something blindly because you haven't had any direct experience. Direct introduction and discovering our real nature mean we have direct experience through our senses, and that through these experiences we discover our real nature.

For example, if I show you an object, you can look at it and know its form and color. Now if I ask you to forget about it, you can't. If I ask you to change your idea about that object, you can't. Why? Because seeing that object is your direct experience. Discovering your real nature is similar to that.

When you are studying in an intellectual way, you are following another person's idea. For example, you can believe your teacher today, but maybe what your teacher says will not be true for you tomorrow. You can always change your ideas. You have this problem because you have not discovered your state. This is the weak point of intellectual study.

DISCOVERY

When you say "discover," it means that you have a precise experience. In particular, when you are following Dzogchen teaching, you must discover your real nature directly, with methods. When you discover your nature, you discover the value of transmission at the same time. In this case, you also discover the principle and function of the teaching. Discovering the principle of the teaching does not mean that you accept or decide something.

In the same way, you discover the value of the teacher through experience, not by deciding that the teacher must be your root master. In general, many people choose a root master perhaps because he or she is very famous, or other people consider that teacher to be very important. And then, even if you don't discover your real nature, you always say, "Oh, this is my root master," but you go to someone else to try to discover it. This is an intellectual way of deciding who your root master is.

NOTHING TO DECIDE

There is nothing to decide in regard to the path, the teaching, or the master. You don't need to decide or accept anything at all. In particular, if you meet a serious Dzogchen teacher, he or she never asks you to accept a teaching, the teacher, or the transmission. The teacher only asks you to discover, and gives you methods. Working together with these methods, you try to discover that. When you have discovered one, you have discovered all. This is the basis of the Dzogchen teaching. If you only open one eye, you can see everything. You don't need to open your eyes one at a time in order to see.

In the Dzogchen teaching it is said that when we discover our real nature, we discover everything. For example, many Dzogchen masters never studied or learned in an intellectual way. When they received a precise transmission, they practiced and used methods, woke up, and became learned and scholarly. It works that way.

The principle is that we try to discover our real nature. To do this, we must first open our eyes, look at our situation, condition, and limitations, and learn in a precise way. You remember the Buddha's teaching on cause and effect. When you discover there is a cause, then you discover that there is also an effect. If you open your eyes without limiting yourself, then you can discover everything—particularly how to work with the teaching, the transmission, and the methods.

6   The Base in Dzogchen[21]

A teacher who is introducing a student to knowledge is introducing what we call in the Dzogchen teaching the Base, or *zhi* in Tibetan: that which we have had since the beginning, our potentiality. If we do not understand the *zhi*, we cannot know what introduction means. A Dzogchen master gives an introduction to the natural state, and people receive the introduction, and, perhaps, enter into that knowledge. This is the Dzogchen point of view.

In Buddhism, we find numerous schools and traditions, and it is useful to learn the important characteristics of their distinctive view-points. In the Sutra teachings of India, many philosophical schools, like the Madhyamika and the Yogachara,[22] have flourished; and in Tibet, among the traditions of Tantric Buddhism, there are different views. The Dzogchen definition of the Base, what we understand to be the underlying reality, is not universally accepted. It is important to know that, so that you are not confused should you one day find a book or some other Buddhist source that negates Dzogchen. That there are different schools of thought is not surprising, because in samsara everyone lives in a dualistic vision, which means having limited points of view. That is normal. Why do some Buddhist teachings negate Dzogchen? The main point of contention is the Base, not the Path or the Fruit.

Dzogchen informs us that the teacher's function is to introduce knowledge. The Sutra teaching, and people who are conditioned by the ideas of Sutra, will never accept this concept; they see nothing to introduce. In Dzogchen, *rigpa* means knowledge of our natural state, the contrary of *marigpa*, which means ignorance of our real nature and potentiality. If you read a book in the Sutra tradition, you will find that *rigpa* means "ordinary intelligence." Also, in spoken Tibetan, children who are clever are said to have "a very good *rigpa*."

Madhyamika

The Sutra teaching has never recognized *rigpa* as explained in the Dzogchen teaching. Why? In Sutra the most important view is that of Nagarjuna, as expressed in Madhyamika philosophy. Sakya Pandita (1182–1251) said that no point of view surpasses Nagarjuna's, because Nagarjuna established the view beyond concepts. If another philosophical position is considered more important than his, that position is necessarily a fixed concept. What does it mean that Nagarjuna's explanation "reached beyond concepts"? With great intelligence he employed logic to reach beyond itself, which is the final goal in Madhyamika. Intellect can go no further.

The Dzogchen knowledge is neither an analysis nor an intellectual path. A Dzogchen teacher introduces methods that you use to have meditative experiences. Through these experiences you discover the real sense of Dzogchen. People who adhere to the ideas of Sutra do not accept that process. In the real sense this is not negative, because Sutra always aims for the understanding or knowledge of *shunyata*.

How can you reach realization if you are not going to have experiences? Madhyamika explains with the four "beyond concepts," which are that something neither exists, nor does not exist, nor both exists and does not exist, nor is beyond both existing and not existing together. These are the four possibilities. What remains? Nothing. Although you are working only in an intellectual way, this can be considered the ultimate conclusion in Madhyamika. As an analytical method, this is also correct for Dzogchen. Nagarjuna's reasoning is supreme.

If you distinguish, however, between the use of a logical system and a method that functions with experience through which you discover your nature, you will see that these methods are radically different. This is why Madhyamika, which is a philosophical system, negates the existence of the Base completely. In Dzogchen, the Base does not mean a concrete object or concept, but rather our real condition. Introduced to your natural state, you become one with that knowledge. That is the meaning of introduction.

YOGACHARA SYSTEM

People who have learned a little about Sutra and then study the Dzogchen teaching often confuse the Base in Dzogchen with the concept of the "base" in the Yogachara system. The Yogachara system uses the term *kunzhi*, *kun* meaning "all," and *zhi* meaning "base." For Yogachara, the *kunzhi* is the base because that is where the potentiality of karma is stored. Traditional Buddhist scholars asked, for example, how seeds of future karmic payment, caused by our actions, mature; how today is connected with that moment in the future when the karmic result manifests;

how the seed is preserved, and why it does not change or lose its capacity. To answer these questions, the Yogachara scholars posited the *kunzhi*, the "base of all," where karma-producing seeds, as potentiality, are maintained. They considered that the base exists for this purpose.

Nagarjuna refuted the Yogachara concept of *kunzhi* and never accepted it. He could not understand the Dzogchen view of the Base, and thus his Madhyamika philosophy rejected that as well. Specifically, Madhyamika does not accept the Yogachara base because if causes for negative karma are created, then, when secondary circumstances arise, karma will inevitably manifest. That potentiality is not something concrete on the material level that can get lost, change, or lose its capacity to manifest. For example, though a physical body can have a shadow, we cannot see the shadow if no secondary cause exists. When a secondary cause like light or sunshine is present, then the shadow appears immediately. So a repository, the Yogachara concept of the base, is not necessary. In short, in the Madhyamika view, when a karmic seed is produced a consequence always follows, but a consequence that manifests only in the presence of secondary causes.

The Madhyamika and Yogachara Schools have different positions on many other points as well. For example, the Madhyamika philosophy speaks of the aggregation of six consciousnesses, whereas for the Yogachara School, and the many Tantric systems linked to it, we possess an aggregation of eight consciousnesses.[23] Reasoning about these distinctions does not mean we are entering into real knowledge in the Dzogchen sense of the term, since such analysis proceeds at the level of mere logic. Of course, logic has its role. If someone is debating and discussing, establishing a point of view, then you must answer appropriately. One person asks, another replies. You cannot respond with a history of your spiritual experiences.

A teaching like Dzogchen, and the principle of Tantra as well, is related to the individual's contemplative or meditative experience. Those who deny Dzogchen are simply following a system of logic, thinking and judging. This attitude does not correspond to the real sense of the teaching, since you cannot realize yourself through intellect alone. Thus, you must distinguish clearly between these two very different approaches, the logical and the experiential. You can begin to move toward realization only through your experience of the state of knowledge.

People who negate Dzogchen often say that the Dzogchen explanation of the Base is influenced by the Yogachara system. In truth, the Dzogchen Base has nothing to do with the Yogachara concept. In Yogachara, the base is related to mind and, therefore, to the intellectual functions, whereas in Dzogchen, the Base is an aspect of our real condition and potentiality.

Some verbal similarities exist between Yogachara and Dzogchen. Yogachara says everything is created by mind, and in Dzogchen, we have the Semde Series of teachings; *sem* or, in Sanskrit, *chitta*, means "mind," but in this context it is referring to the nature of mind. Dzogchen appears to say that everything is somehow a manifestation of mind, and so the two systems seem rather similar; but Yogachara, proceeding in an intellectual way in a series of logical steps, believes that mind creates something.

That is not the Dzogchen view. Instead, Dzogchen states that mind, or the nature of mind, our potentiality, is like a mirror. Reflections appear in a mirror when secondary causes manifest, but this does not mean that the mirror creates what you see. You must grasp this distinction. Everything, good or bad, appears in the mirror, and this mode of manifesting energy is called *rolpa*. *Rolpa* means manifesting in its own dimension. This manifestation occurs because the secondary cause presents itself.

For example, if a dog stands in front of a mirror, then that dog is reflected in the mirror; if there is a statue of Buddha, then a statue of Buddha appears in the mirror. For the mirror there is no difference. Reflections appear because secondary causes are present, but the mirror is not creating the Buddha or the dog. If you understand that distinction, you will comprehend why the Base in Dzogchen has nothing in common with the base as understood in the Yogachara system.

A number of narrow-minded scholars—Kagyüdpas in ancient times and, more recently, some Gelugpas—rejected Dzogchen in many books, which, if they are ever translated, might be available to you some day. Their arguments might cause you to think, "Oh, something is wrong with Dzogchen." Their principal assertion is that the Base as conceived in Dzogchen does not exist. They further declare that the Dzogchen point of view and the texts that explicate it were late and spurious Tibetan inventions, and negate the Dharmakaya origin recorded in the Dzogchen tantras. They thus claim that the *Kunjed Gyalpo* itself, the root tantra of Dzogchen,[24] is a false creation, not a primordial manifestation. By their reasoning, no original Dzogchen books could have existed in ancient times, because these texts cannot be found in the Sanskrit language in India, though it is said that these books were introduced into Tibet from India.

In fact, most Dzogchen books were translated from the Oddiyana language into Tibetan, and not from the Sanskrit, though they may or may not have arrived by way of India. Answering these charges, famous scholars like Longchenpa (1308–1363) and Sodogpa Lodrö Gyaltsen (1552–c.1624) demonstrated, in many volumes, that the refutations of Dzogchen are false, and that such arguments are without foundation. This is all on the level of intellectual proof and argument. Now, centuries later, since the famous Tunhuang documents have been unearthed in China, these debates are no longer to the point, because actual physical evidence, the ancient texts themselves, definitively refute these misunderstandings about Dzogchen.

At Tunhuang, many ancient and important books from the times of the Tibetan kings were discovered, including Tibetan, Chinese, and Uighur texts. Entombed for many centuries, this vast library emerged revealing details of ancient history both spiritual and secular. All scholarly authorities consider these books extremely significant. Among them are two very important ancient Dzogchen texts.[25] With that documentation available, it is not easy to deny the origins of the Dzogchen teaching.

THREE ASPECTS OF THE BASE

In any case, it is important to know what *zhi*, or the Base, signifies in Dzogchen. Understanding the meaning of *zhi* is of particular importance in the Dzogchen teaching. The Base has three aspects: Essence, Nature, and Energy. Its Essence is emptiness; its Nature is clarity; and its Energy is without interruption. Through an understanding of what is meant in this context by "Energy," we can arrive at a definitive knowledge of the inherent potentiality of the individual, which manifests as sound, lights, and rays. This knowledge of the Base and how to work with it are characteristic of the Dzogchen teaching.

ESSENCE

When a teacher gives an introduction to the natural state, he or she brings the person receiving the introduction into a direct experience of the knowledge of the Base. But how can we arrive at knowledge of this

Essence, which is the first of the three aspects of the Base? Essence is emptiness, and to discover it we must experience it ourselves, understanding what it means in terms of our real nature. When we observe our own minds, we notice that an infinite number of thoughts follow each other in continuous succession. If we give our full attention to each thought in turn, observing the first thought, the second thought, and so on, each one disappears of itself, and what we always find is emptiness, nothing concrete. The original texts of Dzogchen affirm in this regard that "finding nothing is the most you can find." Our real condition is emptiness, so what is there to find? Even if we believe there is something to find, there is in fact nothing there. When you discover for yourself that there really is nothing, you have made the greatest discovery.

NATURE

The Nature of this Base is clarity. What does this mean? Though this is a very important point in both Dzogchen and Tantra, it is more difficult to understand in Tantra, because no clear explanation of it is given there. Continuing with the example of how our own thoughts manifest, we can observe that we have an infinite number of thoughts, both good and bad; all these thoughts and all our experiences related to body, energy, and mind are part of our clarity, our nature. This clarity is part of our real condition, which is why we call it "Nature." Essence and Nature are not two separate things, but are two different aspects of our real condition. Explanations such as this are not found at all in the Sutra teachings. The sutras only explain emptiness, and their final goal is the realization of the knowledge of emptiness. Thus, explanations of emptiness are always given, because it is regarded as the most important thing.

In the Dzogchen teachings, emptiness is also considered to be important because it is the Essence, but this Essence is also understood to have its Nature and its Energy. Our real nature is not only emptiness. As Dzogchen practitioners, we must understand this. So the Essence has the aspect of clarity, and we discover that clarity is part of our real nature.

In the Sutra teachings, explanations are given of the two truths, absolute and relative. The term "absolute truth" refers to the state of emptiness. This is the same as what is meant in Dzogchen by the Essence. The term "relative truth," as referred to in the sutras, with its concepts of pure and impure vision, is regarded as being the cause or condition of samsara. It must therefore be renounced, while knowledge of the absolute truth, or nirvana, is regarded as being what one should develop. Thus, in the sutras, the relative condition is considered to be samsara, which must be abandoned. This means that samsara and the relative condition are considered not to be of any value at all.

KUNTUZANGPO, OR SAMANTABHADRA

In the Dzogchen teaching, however, the relative condition is not considered to be wrong or without value. In Sanskrit we use the term *Samantabhadra*, and in Tibetan, *Kuntuzangpo*. *Kuntu* means "everything," *zangpo* means "fine." If you have knowledge, everything is fine. Then there is nothing to reject, nothing that you consider to be without value. Even if it is samsara, that is also fine. Samsara presents no problems if you really have understanding. Samsara only becomes a cause of sorrow and problems when you are conditioned by emotions and everything else. When you don't have real knowledge, then you can no longer speak of Samantabhadra, of everything being fine.

In Dzogchen, samsara, the movement of thought in the mind, and everything that arises in the relative condition are all considered to be part of clarity; it is not necessary that there should be the manifestation of a mandala or a deity. Even karmic vision, which we normally consider a sorrowful condition, is considered to be part of our clarity.

Tantric Transformation

Tantric methods, on the other hand, involve the transformation of impure vision into pure vision, and then the integration of that pure vision into our real condition. The final arrival point of this method is that everything enters into the state of Mahamudra. This involves the idea of pure vision and impure vision, of an ordinary relative condition on one hand and of a valuable relative condition on the other, and the terms *yangdag kundzob* and *logpai kundzob* are used. *Yangdag kundzob* means the pure relative truth; *logpai kundzob* means the opposite, the impure relative condition, which produces negative karma. When you are in the process of realizing Mahamudra in the Tantric system you cannot isolate yourself in the idea of pure vision alone, even if you consider what you experience as pure vision. Otherwise, you will never realize yourself. This is the main point.

In the Dzogchen teaching, impure vision is regarded as part of our clarity. When we practice, our presence includes that knowledge. This means that we experience our real nature. We know that the Essence is our real condition, so we are present in that state, and we know that clarity is our real condition, so we are present in that state. There is no difference.

In the Tantric teachings, there are many transformation practices. These involve thinking, judging, creating mandalas, deities, and so on. How is this done? First of all, we consider everything to be empty of an inherent self-nature, because that is the Base, the Essence. Then we carry out the transformation practice. If there were no emptiness, we could not transform in any way. So we start with this knowledge, imagining that everything is empty, void. Nothing concrete exists. In Yoga Tantra style, all dharmas are considered to be empty, and then the practitioner's idea of emptiness is empowered with mantra so that it becomes something real.

Practice in most traditions, such as Sakyapa, Nyingmapa, and Kagyüdpa, is the same initially. All dharmas are considered to be empty. The mantra is used for empowerment, after which the energy of the elements represented by Ram, Yam, Kham, Lam, and so on is put into action. Then, one by one, the seed syllables of the elements are visualized, and through that the mandala of the elements is manifested. In the mandala they manifest themselves as deities. The mandala of the deities is not considered to be something material, but is rather imagined as a pure dimension with the essence of the five elements. That is how transformation is done. This process involves thinking and judging, so a vision of this kind, an idea of this kind, is necessarily a construction of our mind. That is what is called the pure relative condition. Then, at the end, everything is integrated, and we go beyond even that concept. This is, finally, Mahamudra.

The methods of transformation practice used in the Gelugpa tradition are more or less the same, although some traditions within Gelugpa present the idea of emptiness through a different way of thinking and judging. This is because these streams of Gelugpa tradition consider it dangerous to affirm that everything is emptiness, since they consider that the concrete cannot be totally negated. Instead they say that the nature of everything is emptiness.[26] This is characteristic of the Gelugpa tradition. In any case, the result is still the same.

SAME TASTE

In the Dzogchen teaching, the practitioner knows that all movements of the mind, all circumstances, are part of our clarity. Thus it is not fundamental to the method of Dzogchen to transform bad into good, because in the state of contemplation we are really in the state in which there is no difference between good and bad. In the state of contemplation these opposites have the "same taste." This is also true when the final goal of Tantra—Mahamudra—is reached; good and bad then have the same flavor, just as they do in Dzogchen. Thus, it can be seen that in Dzogchen no great importance is attached to the distinction between pure and impure vision. That is why the method that characterizes the Dzogchen teaching is called self-liberation, and not transformation.

In Tantra there is the idea that something is transformed into something else, and that concept is fundamental to Tantric practice. For that reason, in the Tantric teaching there is always a very precise concept of pure vision and impure vision, and the understanding that impure vision is being transformed into pure vision.

The idea of impure and pure vision is absent right from the beginning in the process of learning about Dzogchen. Of course, the experience of the individual consists of pure and impure vision through the infinite accumulation of karma. Impure vision arises as a consequence of negative karma.

NATURAL STATE

The principle in Dzogchen is knowledge of the natural state. If one has this understanding, everything can be integrated into that state. For that reason, when we do Dzogchen practice, we always speak about integration. "Integration" does not mean putting two things together, or changing some aspects of something. Simply present in the state itself, we do not do anything at all. This is the characteristic method of the Dzogchen teaching, and the real sense of clarity.

In Dzogchen practice, it is not necessary to sit with closed eyes in a one-pointed way as is done in Sutra practice. That is not the principle. We do not consider that contemplation or meditation means remaining in silence. That attitude belongs to the Sutra tradition, which has developed very much everywhere. People have the idea that if someone sits without moving, perhaps with their eyes closed, then they are meditating. Moreover, the person who is doing this also believes that he or she is meditating.

Many Westerners feel that the Tantric teaching is very interesting, but they do not like to practice; in their view it is not really meditation, but is instead only chanting and ritual. Such people do not really know what contemplation is, and consider meditation to be only sitting in silence without moving. The real meaning of meditation or contemplation, as taught by Buddha Shakyamuni, is to dwell in our real nature.

How can we find ourselves in this real nature? Since our real nature is not just emptiness, but also includes clarity and energy, we must find ourselves both in our energy and our clarity. If the nature of our energy is movement, not silence, then how can we be in that nature without moving?

Practicing Dzogchen does not mean just remaining in silence, but also involves moving, integrating with clarity, and integrating with the movement of energy. Thus you can easily understand why, in Tantric practice, there is so much chanting, singing, moving about, and so on, because that involves integration with energy in movement. Sometimes you can find explanations of this in Tantric teachings, but generally it is only applied and not explained, although you can discover and understand the principle if you think about it. In the Dzogchen teachings, these are things to be learned directly.

ENERGY

The third or last aspect of our Base is Energy, or *thugje* in Tibetan. How does our Energy manifest? It manifests without interruption. You can understand "without interruption" by simply observing your own mind. You have a thought, and immediately after that a second thought arises, then a third one, and so on; an infinity of thoughts, without any interruption at all. Our Energy is in fact constantly in motion, like a waterfall.

This continuation is related to our real condition, our inherent potentiality, which manifests as sound, light, and rays. Through this inherent potentiality of ours—the sound, light, and rays—we are able to connect with the transmission and the various methods, and the possibility is created for transforming into the deities and mandalas. When you receive the transmission of a transformation practice during your lifetime, the teaching becomes linked to your real nature through the power of the transmission and the mantras. Then, if you apply this practice, you will have the possibility of having certain meditative experiences, as well as the possibility of total manifestation. If on the other hand you never receive this kind of method or transmission during your lifetime, your capacity will remain limited to just the sound, light, and rays.

To understand this, we can consider the example of a mirror placed inside a box. A mirror has the potential capacity to reflect everything, but if there are no secondary causes, such as in our example of a mirror enclosed in a box, many possible reflections cannot manifest. If, on the other hand, we receive methods and apply them in our real condition, we are then like a mirror in an open place. When there are objects in front of such a mirror, reflections will arise in it. Receiving initiation thus means that we are given the possibility to realize certain results.

Our human condition includes many functions. If, through the power of the transmission, we can put these various functions to use in the practice of certain methods, we will then have the possibility to manifest specific results. This is why, for example, there are both wrathful and peaceful manifestations. The peaceful manifestations represent the inherent condition of our mind as the calm state, through which one can experience emptiness. The mandala of the peaceful manifestations is related to that aspect.

Thus, one aspect of our condition is emptiness; the other is the infinite movement that is our energy. All these movements are related to our senses. For example, with the eye we see objects, with the ear we hear sounds, and so on, which means that through our sense organs we have contact with objects. When we have contact with objects, we immediately enter into judgment and thoughts, and then movement arises. Through the consciousnesses of our senses, we receive information that is finally received by the mind. This movement represents the manifestation of the wrathful aspect.

Peaceful and wrathful manifestations in the *bardo*[27] can only be experienced by people who have received the *bardo* teaching, and who have at least a minimal connection with the transmission. Individuals with that history can have these types of visions in the *bardo* because they have obtained that capacity and created that possibility. If you have never received a teaching of that kind, then, after death, you will only experience the sound, light, and rays, which are in fact the nature, the inherent potentiality, of all sentient beings.

Tsal, Rolpa, and Dang

The Energy of the Base manifests as *Tsal, Rolpa,* and *Dang.* Why does this Energy have these three aspects? In relation to realization there are the three kayas—the Dharmakaya, Sambhogakaya, and Nirmanakaya. The three kayas are related to the three aspects of our condition: Essence, Nature, and Energy. The Essence is emptiness, and knowledge of that is the Dharmakaya of the Base. Dharmakaya, Sambhogakaya, and Nirmanakaya are not only qualities of the Buddha; they are also the potentiality of every individual. How can we discover and understand this for ourselves? We observe ourselves. When you discover your Essence, it means you discover the Dharmakaya of your Base. When you discover your Nature, your clarity, then you discover the Sambhogakaya of your Base. When you discover the uninterrupted continuity of your Energy, you discover the Nirmanakaya of your Base. We have these attributes.

Energy manifests in three different ways as Dharmakaya, Sambhogakaya, and Nirmanakaya. The Dharmakaya aspect is called the *Dang* Energy. *Dang* means that in the state of contemplation, our real condition of the Base, our Energy, manifests in the way a crystal ball does. If a crystal ball is placed on a red surface, it appears red, while on a green surface, it appears to be green, and so on, but in fact its basic condition never changes. That is how the Energy called *Dang* manifests. When we are in a state of contemplation, in whatever circumstances we find ourselves, we are integrated into the state of contemplation. We do not remain apart, thinking that we are in contemplation, and that we do not care about circumstances. Circumstances are integrated, like the example of the crystal ball. That is how *Dang* Energy manifests.

The example of a mirror is used to explain the aspect of Energy called *Rolpa*. Whatever is in front of a mirror, whether good or bad, is immediately reflected in it. The practitioner is not conditioned by what appears in the mirror because he or she understands that whatever appears is only a reflection. Whether the reflections are good or bad is not important because, at the level of the profound meaning, there is no difference between good and bad. The reflections only manifest because of the natural capacity of our condition to reflect. Everything manifests just as it is—color, form, shape, and size—anything can appear. That is the characteristic manifestation of the aspect of Energy called *Rolpa*.

Another manifestation of Energy is called *Tsal*, which is related to the Nirmanakaya condition. The example used in this case is a piece of rock crystal that is struck by the sun's rays. Infinite rainbow colors emanate from such a rock crystal onto the walls of a room in which it is placed, but if you look into the rock crystal you cannot see these rainbows inside it; they are only visible outside. This is the aspect of Energy called *Tsal*.

It is through this *Tsal* Energy that our manifestation of pure and impure vision, and our particular karmic vision, arises. We are now human beings, and we have human vision. We perceive our environment dualistically, splitting it into an apparent reality of a perceiving subject separated from a world of external objects. But in fact everything we perceive is like the rainbow lights, which have their source in the rock crystal when it is struck by the sun's rays. If we see a five-colored rainbow, this means that we perceive the pure dimension, pure vision. When the essence of the elements combines together with our karma, then the elements manifest on the material level, creating impure vision. Thus, the source of karmic vision is this aspect of Energy known as *Tsal*; but this same *Tsal* Energy, through certain practices particular to the Dzogchen teaching, such as Thödgal and Yangti, gives us the possibility of reintegrating our material existence, and of finally realizing the Rainbow Body.[28]

7   Invocation of Samantabhadra[29]

I want to explain the meaning of the Invocation of Samantabhadra[30] contained in an Upadesha tantra. Within this tantra is the very essence of knowledge of the Dzogchen teaching. It has already been translated into English.

This invocation is not only to be used as such, but is very important for having knowledge and understanding. In general, practitioners use this as an invocation—chanting and reciting it in order to be in the state of knowledge. Particularly at the beginning of the invocation, there are verses that are essential Dzogchen.

EVERYTHING HAS THE SAME BASE

The beginning of the first verse says that the Bases of all of the universe, samsara, nirvana, and all our considerations, are the same Base. There is a Tibetan word *zhichig; chig* means "one," *zhi* means "base." One Base does not mean the only Base, but the same Base.

For example, in the universe there are infinite sentient beings, including all enlightened beings. All these beings, whether enlightened or in samsara, have the same Base. One of the most important things we learn in Dzogchen is what the Base is. The Base is our real condition. When we explain the Base, we use the explanation of Essence, Nature, and Energy. Even if we use these different aspects, they are all the Base. There is no difference, enlightened or not. That is why in Dzogchen we say that from the beginning, our state is the enlightened state. Our real Base, or condition, never changes. If we follow the teaching and use methods or practices for purification, we purify obstacles, but that doesn't change our nature. Our real condition is the same Base since the beginning.

TWO PATHS

Lamnyi means there are two paths, or two aspects, of manifestation. When we have knowledge or understanding of the Base, or are in the condition of the Base, we are enlightened, in the state of illumination. If we are ignorant of that and are no longer in that state, then we fall into dualistic vision and samsara.

When did this samsara and nirvana start? In the West we usually have a Judeo-Christian education, and have the idea that someone has created everything from the beginning. Who created this and divided these paths into two? No one divided them. Their division is related to our nature. If we have movement in our nature, it must manifest. If we have the capacity of manifesting reflections, somehow they manifest when circumstances arise.

Samsara has no starting point, because our real condition is beyond time. When we are beyond time, we are in an illuminated state and no longer in samsara; however, we don't remain in that state for a long time, because after a few seconds or minutes, thoughts arise, and we are conditioned by them. If thoughts arise and we do not follow them, this is the state of contemplation. That state of clarity, or "instant presence," is the enlightened state. When we are distracted with thoughts and dualistic vision, we are in samsara. That moment is the starting point of samsara. Tomorrow we can be at the starting point of samsara many times. We can have millions and millions of starting points of samsara. It depends on our condition.

Generally speaking, it is explained that one who is in the state of instant presence from the beginning and is never distracted has knowledge or understanding. That primordial understanding is called Samantabhadra, which is the symbol of the Ati Buddha—the primordial Buddha that since the beginning has never been conditioned by dualistic vision. If we don't have this knowledge or understanding, there is no way we can realize or get into that state.

When we speak of *lamnyi,* or two paths, it means that there are two paths through which samsara and nirvana, the two fruits, or *drebunyi,* are produced. These two fruits depend on whether we have knowledge and understanding or not. Those who have that kind of knowledge are enlightened, and those who are ignorant continually create negative karma and the potentiality of karma, which produce infinite samsara.

RIGPA AND MARIGPA

What is the cause of these two paths and two fruits? Here we arrive at the main point: *rigpa* and *marigpa. Rigpa* means knowing or being in that knowledge and understanding; *marigpa* means ignorance of real knowledge or understanding. If we are ignorant, we fall totally into dualistic vision. The way we fall is very simple. For example, we can relax a bit, and observe our thoughts and circumstances. Our eyes see, our ears hear, all our organs have functions, and immediately we have contact through the senses, and we think and judge. We see something very pleasant, receive the information through our vision, and immediately our judgment arises: "Oh, how nice, I like that." That means we are accepting and creating attachment. Then we fight and struggle to get that object of attachment. When we can't get that object, we suffer. So this is how we fall into suffering.

If we see something we don't like, we say, "Oh, I don't like that, and if you put it in front of me, it makes me nervous." That means we are rejecting and are angry with that object. These are our two main emotions, attachment and anger. In this way we accept and reject over and over again, falling into dualistic vision, and accumulating the negative potentiality of karma. When we produce negative karma, it has the potentiality for producing samsara. Therefore, our obstacles of negative karma become thicker and thicker, and we become more and more ignorant of our condition.

Buddha Essence

Even if we possess our potentiality of self-perfected qualities from the beginning, if we are not aware of it, there is no value. This principle is found not only in Dzogchen, but also in the Sutra teaching. In Sutra it is called "Buddha essence," meaning that everyone has the Buddha essence, and if we make sacrifices and purify ourselves, there is the possibility of realizing Buddhahood. There is a book called *Gyüd Lama,* or *Uttaratantra,*[31] by Maitreyanatha. It explains and gives an example that is very important in the Dzogchen teaching as well. It uses the following example:

74

There was a very poor man living in the country. Every day he went to town to get food. He didn't have a house, and every night he went to a mountain cave to sleep. He passed his life in this way. In front of this mountain there was a practitioner, a yogi, who was doing retreat. Every day, the yogi saw the old man going to town and coming back in the evening. Then the yogi noticed that the old man no longer came out of his cave. He saw by means of his clairvoyance that the old man was dead in the cave. He looked a little deeper with his clairvoyance to discover why and how the old man had died, and he realized that the old man had a negative karma to purify and, due to this, had no money. He also saw that every night, in the place the old man put his head to sleep, there was a big diamond. Even though the old man had touched this diamond every day, he never realized that it was a diamond. If he had discovered this diamond, he would have become very rich.

This is an example of how we each have the Buddha essence, like that diamond. When we don't discover it, even if we have it, it has no value.

DUALISTIC VISION

All our sense organs are directed externally to have contact with objects. When we have this contact with the objects of our senses, we fall into dualistic vision, and have no capacity to observe ourselves. In Dzogchen, therefore, we do not use the teaching and our understanding like eyeglasses, because even if they are clear and strong, they always look outside. We use the teaching and knowledge like a mirror.

If we look in a mirror, we discover how our face appears. In this same way, if we turn our awareness within ourselves, then we can discover and have knowledge, understanding; this is the principle of *rigpa* or *marigpa*—having understanding or not. Whoever has this knowledge can be in their real condition and be like Samantabhadra and Vajrasattva. If we look outside—judging, thinking, and multiplying our dualistic vision—we end up with infinite dualistic vision and samsara.

In the Dzogchen teaching we have a word *rulog,* which means "reverse." Instead of going directly into samsara, we reverse this process and get into real knowledge or understanding.

REALIZATION

Through this invocation we can have this experience and be again in our real potentiality. This is called realization, or enlightenment. Realization or enlightenment is not something we construct or build. If we consider realization as something that we build, then it doesn't correspond; it becomes something made up of aggregates, or something impermanent. If we create something within time and through action, we can never get beyond time. In our real condition, the Base is beyond time, beyond consideration, explanation—beyond everything. That is why, at the end of his life, Buddha Shakyamuni explained everything as emptiness with the teaching of the Prajñaparamita. Even at the end of his life he said there was no wisdom, no path, and no realization. Why did he negate all these things? We always enter into concepts. If we say "wisdom," then we have a concept, and if we remain in this concept, we have a problem. Realization must be beyond all this. Even in the Sutra teaching Buddha explained things in that way.

SELF-PERFECTION

In Dzogchen we have the quality of self-perfection from the beginning. It doesn't mean that something has been built and then qualified, but rather the nature of our real condition. For example, in the summer there are many kinds of flowers and trees in the garden. No one made them. The self-perfection of everything is our qualification. This is the Base in the real sense.

Why do we say that the Base, or Essence, is empty? Because when we search there is nothing to find. We always reach the point of emptiness; our real condition is emptiness. If we are in a room at night and the room is totally dark, in whatever direction we move, we will reach a wall. Rooms have walls; we can't reach beyond, and we accept that. Similarly, we are always in our real nature of emptiness. When we search, we always find emptiness; and reaching this emptiness, we discover our condition.

Although we only find emptiness, our real condition is emptiness with infinite potentiality. This is not just an idea of emptiness, such as the idea of horns on a hare or a horse. These animals don't have horns, but you can imagine they do, even though in reality they have never existed. Although this is a kind of emptiness, it has no function.

EMPTINESS WITH INFINITE POTENTIALITY

The emptiness that has no function is not the same as the total emptiness of our real nature, the Dharmata or Dharmakaya. This is emptiness that can have infinite manifestations. We can observe the emptiness of space and the infinite manifestations of this dimension. When we gaze in the sky there may be nothing there; however, when clouds arise, those manifestations cannot be separated from the space of the sky; they manifest in the same dimension as space. In the same way, emptiness has infinite potentiality, and for that reason we say that our Nature is clarity. Even if it is empty, through its natural clarity it manifests everything as Energy without interruption. With this knowledge of Essence, Nature, and Energy we can understand the three dimensions—Dharmakaya, Sambhogakaya, and Nirmanakaya. In the pure dimension we say Dharmakaya, Sambhogakaya, and Nirmanakaya. When we have this knowledge of Essence, Nature, and Energy we have the understanding of the three dimensions.

THREE KAYAS

In the teaching there is an explanation of the three dimensions, the three kayas of the Base, Path, and Fruit. If you read many books, particularly Mahayana texts, then you understand that these three kayas explain some qualities of enlightened beings. In the real sense, it is not only the explanation of enlightened beings, but also the explanation of our condition. It is very important to know this from the beginning. Essence is empty, and is Dharmakaya. Nature is clarity, and means manifestation, and is Sambhogakaya. And Energy without interruption means Nirmanakaya. When we are in a state of contemplation, we are in those three states. When we have that knowledge through introduction, we have discovered our real Base. How we manifest this concretely depends on how we do practice and how we realize.

Discovering our real nature doesn't mean we manifest our qualities. In the Dzogchen teachings there is the example of the practitioner's knowledge, which is similar to the egg of the eagle. The egg of the eagle is different from other eggs; when it opens, the small eagle is perfectly formed and ready to fly, self-perfected from the beginning. That is why it is said to be like a practitioner of Dzogchen. Even if we live with the limitation of the physical body, our capacity, knowledge, and under-standing are perfected. When we liberate from this physical body, we have the realization of all three kayas.

8 Contemplation in Dzogchen[32]

There are various experiences that form the basis for the development of contemplation. They are considered to be very important topics, and it is important to understand why.

SUTRA: SHINE AND EMPTINESS

If we are following the methods of the Sutra level of the teachings, the practice that is most commonly used in order to begin the process of bringing the practitioner into the state of the nature of mind is called Shine, a practice through which we seek to develop a state of meditative calm. Shine is discussed and practiced a great deal in many different traditions, and some traditions consider it to be the principal point of meditation; however, one must not forget that this understanding of Shine is essentially the point of view of Sutra, a point of view that is not shared by other levels of the teachings.

The practice of Sutra is generally always more related to the physical level, and the fundamental principle behind the methods of the Sutra teachings is that of controlling our three existences of body, voice, and mind in such a way that we avoid committing any negative actions, and only perform positive ones. In the Sutra methods, we govern our behavior by maintaining various vows that we have taken, and by following rules connected to them that we have vowed to abide by.

Beyond following rules and vows, when followers of the Sutra system practice to attain realization and develop deeper knowledge, they practice Shine. Why do they start with Shine? The fact is, we live in the relative condition, in the midst of great confusion, and as a result of all this we develop many mental problems. So the first thing we need to do is to discover and enter a calm state of mind. That is the reason for the existence of the method known as Shine.

When we apply Shine, we can find ourselves in a calm state. Then, as a result of having calmed our minds, we can discover the experience of emptiness. But when we learn Shine in the style of Sutra, it is often the case that much more emphasis is placed on discovering the calm state, and there is relatively little explanation or importance given to the experience of emptiness. Why is this? It is simply a characteristic of certain styles of Sutra teaching. But if you are learning a teaching like Dzogchen, then you should understand what the purpose of Shine is. The final goal of Shine is to enable us to enter into the experience of emptiness.

Fixation with an Object

To arrive at this experience, we begin our practice of Shine with fixation, fixing our eyes on an object such as a statue of the Buddha, or a *thangka*, such as a painting of Mañjushri, or a small piece of wood or stone. A style of fixation that is characteristic of Dzogchen is to use the letter *A* as the object of fixation. In any event, we place an object in front of us, and fix our gaze and our attention on it one-pointedly.

Why do we practice Shine using an object in this way? We live in a dualistic condition, and are very used to the objects of dualistic perception. If we don't have something concrete in front of us, it is harder for us to do the practice. This is why we use an object. By fixing our attention on an object one-pointedly, we can control the constant habitual chatter of our minds, and finally enter the calm state. We practice Shine in that manner, and we gradually arrive at a calm state. When we can remain in a calm state for a longer period of time, even though thoughts arise, we are realizing the practice of Shine.

FIXATION WITHOUT AN OBJECT

Then we train in the practice of Shine without using an object as the basis for the fixation of our gaze and attention. We take away the object, and at this point we gaze into space, into the dimension of emptiness. Keeping all our senses quiet, we try to relax into the same calm state that we arrived at through fixation using an object. This second phase of Shine practice is called "fixation without an object." In any case, we consider that we have succeeded in our practice of Shine when we can remain for a longer period of time without thoughts, in a state of one-pointed attention without being disturbed in any way by thoughts. In that state of one-pointed attention, we discover that the real, inherent condition of the calm state is emptiness. We are actually experiencing the emptiness of all phenomena for ourselves. This is one kind of experience.

It is generally quite easy to arrive at this experience of the emptiness of all phenomena. What is more difficult to understand is the discovery, when we find ourselves in the calm state, that our real nature comprises not only the calm state, but also the infinite movements of thought related to our emotions and to our energy that arise continually as the function of the state of emptiness.

TANTRA–INTEGRATING WITH MOVEMENT

In the Tantric and Dzogchen teachings, there are specific instructions and methods that work specifically with this movement that do not rely only on remaining or resting in the calm state.

When the condition of the individual is explained in the teachings in general, we speak of *nepa* and *gyuwa*. *Nepa* refers to the calm state; *gyuwa* refers to the aspect of our condition as movement. In the calm state we discover this movement of our thoughts, emotions, and energy, and then we must integrate with it. There are various methods we can receive to integrate with this movement, but such methods are not found in the Sutra teachings. They are, however, the principal method used in Tantra.

That is why Tantric methods involve chanting, singing, the use of instruments, and various different types of movements. People who are not accustomed to doing these types of things do not consider this to be meditation. They say, "Oh, I like to practice meditation, but I don't like to do pujas, rituals." Or, "I don't like to perform Tantric ceremonies." Many people say this sort of thing. But what such statements generally mean is that those who make them do not understand the way in which movement is part of our nature; they don't understand the value of movement. They believe that our condition is emptiness, and that to be in emptiness is everything. But that is not the totality of our real condition. People who make such statements are accustomed to following only Sutra teachings and have no knowledge of the function of Tantric teachings.

TRANSFORMATION

In the Tantric teachings we first receive initiation and instruction. What initiation really means is that we receive information about how to get into a state of transformation; we transform our impure dualistic condition into a pure dimension. What do we mean exactly by transformation? What we are referring to is working with the movement of thought, emotion, and energy that I have just described as being one aspect of the individual's condition, rather than just remaining in the condition of emptiness, which is the other aspect of that condition. By working with this movement we actively transform.

In considering our real condition as a whole, we must first understand its essential emptiness; but our real condition is not only that of emptiness. If our real condition were only empty, and did not also have as its inherent quality the potentiality for infinite manifestation, then that emptiness in itself would be of no value. Since our real condition includes the potentiality for infinite manifestation arising as a quality of the state of emptiness itself, even if we have practiced Shine for a long time, we will not have developed by this means alone the capacity to integrate the movement aspect of our nature. When practitioners of Shine finish their practice and leave the meditation hall, they are often completely distracted by everything that they encounter, because now they are no longer in the calm situation that supported their Shine meditation, and many movements arise that must be dealt with and integrated into practice. Practitioners who are

habituated to Shine might have no capacity to integrate with movement because they lack the necessary experience and only have experience of being in the calm state.

If we are in the calm state, what should we do to develop the
experience of integration? If some movement arises, the first thing we
must do is to notice it. If we walk about, moving around and doing
something, then at that moment we should continue to remain in the
one-pointed state, without distraction. If we are only used to doing
Shine, we will not be able to integrate in this way.

In the Tantric teachings we must have the knowledge of emptiness, because that is indeed our real nature; but then we must also
work with movement, because that is the other aspect of our own
nature. We therefore visualize or imagine that we have transformed
into a particular deity. The various Tantric divinities are personified
forms of different functions of our own energy. We must also understand that our own dimension is a pure dimension, and that our own
situation is in fact a mandala. The details of the deity and the mandala
will have been transmitted to the student by the master who gave the
Tantric initiation for the practice of the divinity that the student is
visualizing.

Through the transmission from the master, and by means of his or
her practice, the student is enabled to enter into the pure dimension
of the mandala—which is in fact the individual's own condition from
the beginning. The means by which this transformation is carried out
is through the movement aspect of one's own energy. The fact is that
whether one is in the state of this movement, or in the calm state in
which there is no movement, there is ultimately no difference between
these two states. They are both aspects of our own condition, a condition that is essentially nondual.

MAHAMUDRA

When you understand this, and actually experience the calm state and movement as being the same, or as aspects of the same indivisible principle, that is the real Mahamudra. It does not mean only being in a state of emptiness.

When we speak of being in the state of Mahamudra, this means that we find ourselves in the state of transformation, in the state of clarity in which we are no longer judging, thinking, creating, or blocking anything. In this state we have the complete capacity to remain integrated in whatever movement arises, whether we are walking, working, or carrying out any kind of activity. All our activities become Mahamudra.

You have read one of the songs of Milarepa in which he sings, "When I go to fetch water, what is it that I am doing? Fetching water is Yantra for me! When I rise from sleep, what is it that I am doing? Rising from sleep is Yantra."

When we practice at this level, all our activities become Yantra, and no other Yantra is necessary. Why does all our activity become Yantra? For a practitioner at this level, every activity is governed by knowledge of how to remain in the state of integration. What we learn in Tantra is to know the value of movement, and how to incorporate movement into the practice of contemplation.

RIGPA, THE STATE OF INSTANT PRESENCE

The Tibetan word for the calm state is *nepa*, and the word for movement is *gyuwa*. But there is a third term that is also used together with these two, and that is *rig*, which generally means "knowledge" or "understanding." But what is being referred to by *rig* is not merely an intellectual understanding, but rather an experiential state of knowledge. I therefore generally translate *rig* as "instant presence." When a state of knowledge is presented in the manner characteristic of Dzogchen, that which is introduced is this instant presence. And when we speak of contemplation, what we are speaking of is being in this state of instant presence, which is generally referred to as *rigpa.*

The term *rigpa* can be used nowadays to mean various different aspects, and is sometimes used in a more general sense to mean "intelligence." But *rigpa* as used in the Dzogchen teachings doesn't just mean ordinary knowledge or intelligence. What is being referred to is an experience. When we have an experience of this instant presence for ourselves, we can recognize it. Then we can really know what is meant by *rigpa.*

We can see that to learn or apply the practice of Dzogchen, or to be in the real state of Dzogchen, the principle is not only that we sit quietly somewhere practicing Shine. Shine is useful and important, but it is not of ultimate importance. Shine, or the state of emptiness, is ultimately only a kind of experience. And in the Dzogchen teachings, there are methods that are much more important than ordinary Shine. People generally do not understand these things. When they speak about Shine, they talk as if they consider it to be a supreme practice. But this is simply not true.

DIRECT INTRODUCTION

In Dzogchen, introduction is spoken of a great deal. When we talk about introduction, what is called direct introduction is considered to be the most important. As a result, some people always seem to be waiting for this direct introduction to arrive from somewhere. Sometimes people come to me and say, "Could you please give me the direct introduction?," as if it were something I keep in my pocket, and that I could just give them. But direct introduction cannot be given that way. It is very important to understand what direct introduction is and how we can have it. When we know the value of experience and understand how to use that experience, then we already have one of the qualifications for receiving direct introduction. Then we need to know how to work with the master, actively participate, and have devotion, so that we are able to work with the master until we reach total realization. Proceeding in this way, we can receive direct introduction.

Sometimes when people learn a particular method, they think to themselves, "Oh, now I understand this method; now I can use it." They write the practice down and go away, not caring very much about the master and the transmission. But this is the wrong way. You need the master until you attain total realization. You also need to work with the master. Spiritual teachings such as those found in Dzogchen are not mere techniques. The tendency to regard the teachings as nothing more than techniques is a pervasive problem among Westerners.

THE IMPORTANCE OF THE MASTER

The master is of paramount importance, because the methods used must be related to the experience of the students. A serious teacher of Dzogchen must understand the experience of any particular student, and then be able to suggest practices according to the way in which that individual is developing, not just give practices according to a set formula regardless of the character, capacity, and progress of each student. We don't need a master if we are just going to go about applying things in a mechanical way. If that were enough, it would also be enough just to read books. We would not need a teacher if we were just applying a set system in the same manner in all circumstances and under all conditions. If, on the other hand, we want to apply the practice according to our own needs and capacities, then the participation of a master is essential. If we need a teacher, it means that teacher and student work together. I have taught this way for many years. If we understand the value of the teaching and the transmission, we understand the importance of the master. If we do not understand these things, then we will think that it is enough to first do this, and then to do that, as if we were working with a computer. But teaching must not be applied in such a mechanistic way. The teaching must be understood to be a living force, something that must be kept alive in and between the individuals who practice it. This means that we must work with the teacher and the transmission at all times and without interruption.

People may sometimes feel that they have a problem because their teacher is not physically present with them. We cannot spend all our time with our teacher. In fact this should not become a problem. The point is not that you always need the teacher nearby. It's true that you may sometimes need to ask the master something, but these days there are many possible ways of communicating with the master. If the teacher is still alive, it is always possible to meet with him or her at some point. If you are really practicing seriously, you can, no matter what the situation, maintain communication with the teacher; because when you enter the practice and become a good practitioner, the teacher is found within you. The teacher is not only an external phenomenon. He or she can also manifest through your own clarity. We must have a clear understanding of this. The reality of our actual situation is that everything is not just external to us.

9 Introduction and Knowledge in Tregchöd[33]

When we are following a teaching like Dzogchen, the first thing we need is direct introduction, which means we discover what Dzogchen is. Dzogchen is not a book, a school, or a tradition. Many people think that Dzogchen is a kind of philosophy, but it is not. Dzogchen is our real nature. The first thing we need is to discover our real nature, and that is called introduction. When we say "introduction," it seems that there is something to introduce. Sometimes we remain fixed in this idea, but in the real sense, our potentiality—our nature of mind—is beyond concepts and examples. How can we introduce it? It is not something we introduce like an object. But even if there is nothing concrete to introduce, introducing means we give methods to be able to experience our real nature. When we have experiences, then we can feel and discover our potentiality. After having discovered that, we can say, "The teacher introduced."

The principle of the Dzogchen teaching is not the idea that we are accepting something. We often have this idea. When we follow any teaching, we have the idea, "Now I am becoming someone, I am accepting this method, this teaching, this transmission." That is relative; in the real sense, if you decide to "accept" something, or you have changed and you are "becoming" something or someone, that is false. There is nothing to change, for even if you can change today, tomorrow you can change again.

There are many people who say, "I used to be a Muslim, then I became a Hindu, and today I am becoming a Buddhist." They feel that they have changed. But if you believe that changing in this way is the principle, then today you might be a Buddhist, but tomorrow you might become a Muslim—why not? You can always change—just like your clothes. When you feel too hot, then you need a very thin garment. When you feel cold, you need warm clothes. So you change according to the circumstance. We are playing with our minds and we believe it, but this is false.

ROOT GURU

This is not real knowledge. If we say that we have discovered Dzogchen, it does not mean that we are accepting something. Knowledge of Dzogchen means that we have discovered our nature, and that means remembering the difference between discovering and merely "accepting" something, two completely different ideas. The principle is discovery. You discover the teacher and the qualification of the teacher. Then you discover the transmission and the qualification of the transmission. You discover there is nothing to change.

Some people say, for example, "You are a very good teacher. I want you to be my root Guru." This point of view is really mistaken, because being a root Guru means that a teacher communicates with you and that you wake up and discover your real nature through this teacher and this transmission. In this case, even if you do not accept this teacher, or you have decided that this teacher is not your root Guru, there is nothing to do. He is your root Guru. Even if he is a dog, he is your root Guru! Even if he doesn't sit on a high throne, or dress nicely, or if he is not a very famous teacher, it does not matter.

If you choose someone as your root Guru, saying, "Oh this is a very famous teacher and everybody is saying that this is an enlightened being—wonderful!" and then you say, "Oh, this is my root Guru," even though you did not experience him that way, that is totally false. Why is he your root Guru? Perhaps you never received a single teaching—how can he then be your root Guru? You see, in society we don't understand what it means to be a Guru. It means teaching and giving transmission. That is why, in the Dzogchen way, we need to discover everything; we don't need to decide anything at all. As to the value of the teaching, you say, "Dzogchen is a wonderful teaching," but this does not mean anything. Dzogchen is interesting or powerful or important only if through it you wake up to discover your real nature. Then you find that Dzogchen has a real function.

DISCOVERY

It is very important, when we are following a teaching, particularly Dzogchen, that we understand what "Dzogchen" actually means. Otherwise, year after year passes, but we always remain at the same point. We depend on name and form, but then we continually delude ourselves because it does not correspond to the real sense. A Dzogchen teacher never asks you to accept or change anything. A teacher of Dzogchen only asks that you observe yourself so that you can discover your real nature. If you discover your real nature, that benefits you, not your teacher. The teacher tries to make you understand by giving teachings. We say that the teacher is working with the student to make him or her understand. That is real teaching. If we work that way, then, even if we have only been following the teaching for a short time, it makes sense. If you have not already discovered your real nature and potentiality, maybe through this principle you can discover for yourself one day.

Although the teacher gives many methods in order to have different experiences, first we need knowledge—understanding what it means to be in our real nature. We must discover it; otherwise, we cannot be in that state. This is the first step. After that, we must realize that knowledge so that it becomes real, because although sometimes experience is real, and could be something related to our real nature, we still live in a state with our dualistic views and concepts of subject and object, and possess an infinite potentiality of negative karma.

You can speak about *shunyata*, emptiness, and you can know what it means, and you can also believe that you really know what *shunyata* means; but when you are thinking that everything is *shunyata* and someone hits you, at that moment you experience pain, not *shunyata*. It does not correspond. Why do you have this problem? Because you are not realized. Realization means not only thinking with the mind, but thinking that corresponds with your experience. For that reason we need different kinds of practice. After we have discovered our real nature, there are many methods for realizing it.

TREGCHÖD

In Dzogchen, we are learning primarily methods of practice. In the

Dzogchen Upadesha teachings, for instance, we speak about Tregchöd and Thödgal. These are very famous terms. Tregchöd and Thödgal are special names used only in Upadesha, not in the other Dzogchen teachings. We never use Tregchöd and Thödgal in Dzogchen Semde or in Dzogchen Longde.

But what does Tregchöd really mean? It means that you are totally relaxed. But where and how? You are totally relaxed in your knowledge, the understanding about your real nature that you have already discovered. If you have never discovered it, then where do you relax? What do you relax? There isn't much sense to it. You think, "Oh, I am totally relaxed." That means that you are not doing anything else other than sleeping and eating. Tregchöd doesn't mean that. Tregchöd means that you already have knowledge and understanding. You know, and then you totally relax your body, speech, and mind, and all tensions into that state of awareness.

The Dzogchen Upadesha often refers to the method of Tregchöd, because in the Dzogchen Upadesha the principle is to continue in the state of your knowledge. That is the main point of Dzogchen Upadesha. Of course, in the Dzogchen Upadesha there is also introduction, and then, having had the experience of introduction, you continue, relaxed, in that state.

That is what Tregchöd really means. If you are going somewhere, you can apply the state of contemplation. For instance, when walking, you can relax in the knowledge of your real nature. It isn't necessary to think that in order to apply Tregchöd you must only sit somewhere. You can walk. If you are eating, you must not be distracted, and you must integrate taste and everything else into that state. This means, in other words, that you are relaxed when you are eating, sleeping, or working—at every moment. That is really Tregchöd.

SELF-PERFECTED STATE

People are very attracted to names. They think, "Oh, I really want to learn Tregchöd. It is important." But Tregchöd is important only if you have knowledge. Then you can always integrate your experiences with awareness. For example, in the Dzogchen Semde Series we explain the four states of contemplation, or the Four Yogas.[34] The final state is called the state of *lhundrub*—the self-perfected state. Just that is Tregchöd. There is no difference between the state of *lhundrub* and the Tregchöd spoken of in the Dzogchen Upadesha. However, in the Dzogchen Semde, the term "Tregchöd" isn't used. People use many different names and sometimes names become elegant. We say that the Upadesha teaching is very high, and that Tregchöd, even if we don't know what it is, must be something wonderful, something very elevated. We need to explain what Tregchöd is, because many people don't know its meaning. The real sense of Tregchöd is "total relaxation."

TOTAL RELAXATION

In Tibetan, the word *treg* means "to bind something." If you bind wood, we say *shingtreg*. If you bind clothes or objects, we can use the word *tregpo*, "binding." In general we say our condition is bound up with our tensions, emotions, and confusion. Our body, speech, and mind are all bound up with different kinds of tensions. *Chöd* refers to something that has already been cut, not to something that we are actively cutting. *Chöd* means something already cut loose—freed.

We also have the practice of Chöd. In this case, *chöd* (*gcod*) is a different word, and means "actively cutting"; we are doing a visualization in which we are using methods to cut our ego. But when we say *tregchöd*, *chöd* (*chod*) does not mean that we are actively cutting something, but that something has been cut automatically.[35] If we have discovered our real nature and we are in that state, then we have self-liberation; but it is not that someone is coming and liberating us. That is why we say self-liberation.

SELF-LIBERATION

Self-liberation is like a mirror. If there is a mirror, then, in that mirror infinite reflections can manifest, good or bad. If we are living in dualistic vision, then when we are in front of a mirror we might think, "I am here, the mirror is there, and I am looking in the mirror, and I can see this or that." When you see something nice you are happy: "Oh what a nice thing—I like it, I am enjoying it." But if you see horrible things in the mirror continually for hours and hours, then you become nervous and say, "I don't like it—please take this mirror away." Why? Because you are living in a state of dualistic vision, and have concepts of subject and object when you are looking in the mirror. You have a problem. That is not self-liberation. In this case, if you want to liberate actively, then you do something, like remove the mirror. Although at that moment you no longer have the problem, that is definitely not liberation.

When we say "self-liberation" it means we are not in the state of dualistic vision, but we are being just what we see. If we see the mirror, then the mirror is our condition. We are the mirror. If we are really being the mirror, whether good or bad appears in the mirror, it doesn't matter, because manifestations of reflections are just qualities. There isn't any problem.

CRYSTAL BALL

It is not necessary for us to apply some antidote in order to be liberated or to overcome our problems. When we say Tregchöd it means being in that knowledge and understanding. We are something like a crystal ball. If there is a crystal ball, from the beginning it was pure and clear—that is the quality of a crystal ball. In the same way, we have our real quality in our three primordial wisdoms—Essence, Nature, and Energy. We are being in that knowledge.

In this case, we are like a crystal ball that never changes its nature, quality, or essence. There is nothing to change or develop. Yet it can integrate in any circumstance. You can put a crystal ball on a red table and the ball looks red; on a green base, it appears green; on a multicolored base, multicolored. The crystal ball itself never changes. In the same way, when we are in that state of knowledge and understanding, then even if we are walking, standing, sleeping or eating, it does not matter. Everything is part of that real nature.

10 Dzogchen Longde[36]

Dzogchen Longde was transmitted by Garab Dorje. The Dzogchen Longde root text was called the *Longchen Rabjam Gyalpoi Gyüd*, the *Tantra of Infinite Space*. This is the root tantra of Dzogchen Longde, which was transmitted originally by the teacher Ngöndzog Gyalpo (one of the last of the twelve primordial teachers), whose Nirmanakaya manifestation existed some five thousand years before Buddha Shakyamuni.[37] It's a very ancient teaching that did not exist during the time of Buddha Shakyamuni. The only transmissions that remained at the time of the Buddha were a few oral teachings.

NYENGYÜD AND TANTRAS

The term *nyengyüd* means oral transmission condensed into a few words. There are many teachings called *nyengyüd*, particularly in the modern Bön tradition. Some Lamas and practitioners have visions of teachers, and then they receive teachings from the visions; the Bönpos called it *nyengyüd*. In the Nyingmapa and other traditions, this kind of revelation is called *tagnang*, or pure vision.

In many Buddhist schools the *nyengyüds* were considered something very secret and important, not to be diffused amongst all people. It had to be taught in a limited way. Although there may have been a text, the method of teaching was very secret and limited. Therefore today we have a little confusion; when we say *nyengyüd* we don't really understand the meaning.

In the Dzogchen teaching the word *nyengyüd* has a very precise meaning. In ancient times, not only Ngöndzog Gyalpo taught, but also, even before him, many teachers gave different teachings and tantras. These teachers lived in very ancient times, and did not live only in the human dimension. Then, slowly, the teaching disappeared because the times and circumstances changed. Many teachers also lived and transmitted in the human dimension. After Ngöndzog Gyalpo there was only Buddha Shakyamuni.

There have been many, many changes in the world. After thousands and thousands of years everything has changed, and all the teachings have disappeared. Even though most of the teachings have disappeared, some *nyengyüds* still remain. For example, in the Tantra of Mañjushri there is the phrase *yeshe migchig drima med,* one of the original *nyengyüds*. Even though there is no book, since it has disappeared, this phrase in the Tantra of Mañjushri is the kind of *nyengyüd* that people, particularly practitioners, can keep in their memory.

Some practitioners kept these concise teachings in memory during times when it was not easy to speak the teachings or give transmissions and explanations. They secretly knew these few words, which were like a key. The *nyengyüd* is sometimes a string of words such as *yeshe migchig drima med.* The word *yeshe* means "wisdom," *mig* means "eye"; *migchig* means "unique eye." Thus the phrase translates as "the unique eye of wisdom is pure," which means that the unique eye of wisdom is our consciousness, the nature of mind, our potentiality.

These words are like a key that the teacher would give to those students who were really interested. He would tell them to remember these words, *yeshe migchig drima med*, and give them some practice associated with that *nyengyüd* in order to go more deeply into the meaning.

BÖN

In the time of Garab Dorje there were many *nyengyüds*—oral transmissions that were not taught by Buddha Shakyamuni, but were taught, for example, in the Dzogchen teaching of the Bön. When I say the Bön had Dzogchen teachings, most Buddhists get very upset. They criticize me: "Oh, you are saying that the origin of Dzogchen is Bön, because Bön preceded Buddhism." It doesn't mean that. Originally, Dzogchen was not presented the way Bönpos present it today. Today they teach Dzogchen Semde, Longde, and Upadesha. They not only teach Dzogchen, but they also present Tantra, Prajñaparamita, and everything else. That is modern Bön, not authentic Bön. However, in the authentic Bön there is a *nyengyüd* called *Shang Shung Nyengyüd*. There are twelve specific *nyengyüds*—verses that communicate the Base, Path, and Fruit, as well as the *Tawa, Gompa,* and *Chödpa*—point of view, meditation, and behavior, and how one must apply these.

There were many of these *nyengyüds* also in the time of Garab Dorje. We continue to use these *nyengyüds* today, particularly when we transmit Dzogchen Semde. Although many *nyengyüds* still exist, the original books have disappeared. In regard to the history of Dzogchen, we consider there are thirteen solar system-like dimensions called *thalwas*[38] in which there are Dzogchen teachings, Dzogchen tantras, Dzogchen Rigdzins, or realized beings, and so on. Although there are many existing Dzogchen tantras, we don't have all of them on the planet Earth. Maybe we have sixty or seventy main Dzogchen tantras. Although thousands of original Dzogchen tantras exist in different dimensions of the universe, during the time of Garab Dorje here on Earth, Dzogchen teachings had disappeared, and the only thing that remained were these *nyengyüds*.

Garab Dorje

Garab Dorje is considered a manifestation of Buddha Shakyamuni, because the Buddha gave some indications that in the future there would be a teacher who would transmit a teaching that was beyond cause and effect. Furthermore, in many Dzogchen tantras it is revealed that Garab Dorje is an emanation of Vajrasattva and Vajrapani.

For that reason, Garab Dorje is not an ordinary person, a child who followed a teacher and then did meditation and became enlightened. When Garab Dorje was five or six years old, before he lost his baby teeth, he was always chanting a root Dzogchen tantra called *Dorje Sempa Namkha Che,* one of the most important in the Dzogchen Semde. It is not a very long tantra, but it is considered one of the most important. *Dorje Sempa* in Tibetan means Vajrasattva in Sanskrit. The meaning of Vajra is our real condition, and therefore Vajrasattva means our primordial state. *Namkha che* means total space. That is the total integration of the universe, everything, and everyone in their real, self-perfected state. This is the title of the tantra that this small child Garab Dorje was chanting. Therefore we can understand that he was not an ordinary child.

When Garab Dorje was seven years old, he told his mother that he wanted to have discussions with Buddhist teachers, the royal teachers of the King of Oddiyana. His mother told him it wasn't possible. "You still have your baby teeth, you are very young; it is impossible for you to argue with all these teachers," she said. Many teachers were surprised and curious, and were listening when Garab Dorje chanted this tantra. They were surprised, and some were upset, because this tantra does not speak of the gradual path, or of cause and effect and so on. It explains something beyond cause and effect as well as the real nature. People worried that it could be a very dangerous teaching, contrary to the way of Buddhism, since the Buddha taught in a gradual way about karma, cause and effect, receiving vows, following them, and controlling our existence. All of this is different from the principle of Dzogchen.

MAÑJUSHRIMITRA

The fame of this small child, Garab Dorje, spread to India. In that period, there was a very famous university called Nalanda University, where there were many pandits and learned people. They received this news, and they too were worried. Here is this small child chanting this tantra, already an anomaly, and the meaning is beyond cause and effect. In response they said, "We must check and control this small child, otherwise it could be very dangerous!"

After talking amongst themselves, a group of these pandits, including one of the most important Nalanda pandits, Mañjushrimitra, as well as the pandit Rajahasti, traveled together to distant Oddiyana to meet Garab Dorje. When they met him, they started to argue with Garab Dorje in a philosophical debate style. Garab Dorje replied with only a few words, and Mañjushrimitra, who had a very good connection, perhaps from a previous life, understood immediately what the teachings of Garab Dorje meant, and really woke up. Immediately he became

Garab Dorje's student; and instead of debating with him, became the leader of the group. Then all of the scholars and pandits in the group became students of Garab Dorje. Instead of returning to Nalanda, they remained for a long time in Oddiyana. Garab Dorje's first teachings were transmitted to Mañjushrimitra, who became one of his most important students, and to the others in this group.

Mañjushrimitra was very upset, and regretted his bad intention when he had first approached Garab Dorje. He felt badly about thinking there was something wrong with Garab Dorje, and for his initial intention only to argue with him. Mañjushrimitra, regretting his behavior, wanted to know how to purify the bad actions he had accumulated. Garab Dorje told him not to worry, that he was one of the best pandits, particularly in the Yogachara School of that period, and said that he must write a book explaining Dzogchen through the language of Yogachara, and thereby communicate the Dzogchen principle and knowledge through Buddhist philosophy.

Mañjushrimitra, in order to purify his bad intentions and actions, wrote a book called *Dola Ser Shun*, a text that is considered very important, something like a tantra. When we are learning Dzogchen Semde, we consider it to be one of the most important texts. If you read and study it, it is not so easy to understand because it is written in very philosophical Yogachara language. It is an important book, and has been translated into English by Kennard Lipman, with whom I collaborated.[39]

Mañjushrimitra spent his whole life following and receiving Dzogchen teachings from Garab Dorje. Garab Dorje was a Nirmanakaya manifestation—not just an ordinary scholar—who repeated and taught all the tantras that existed in ancient times but had disappeared from the Earth. Mañjushrimitra and other students wrote them down, and that is why we have some of these tantras today.

LUNG

We do, however, have what are called *lungs*. *Lungs* in this case refer to some chapters that include the main points of the tantras. Some were introduced by Garab Dorje, and then later others were introduced by Mañjushrimitra, Jñanasutra, and Shri Simha, all of whom were realized beings in the state beyond time. They were able to have contact with *Rigdzins*, realized beings from other dimensions. They also had the power to remain in other dimensions. To be able to exist in another dimension we must have realization; then we can be beyond time and distance, and anything is possible.

Realized beings on this level had the capacity to introduce some chapters of the tantras. They couldn't introduce all of them in complete form, but they somehow presented the essential points of these tantras. These texts are called *lungs*.

PADMASAMBHAVA AND SHRI SIMHA

The Dzogchen teaching was originally taught in Tibet by Guru Padmasambhava.[40] Guru Padmasambhava received mainly Dzogchen Upadesha teachings from Shri Simha, his main teacher. Historically, Guru Padmasambhava had eight manifestations, the history of which is a little difficult to understand.

As I understand it, Guru Padmasambhava had different manifestations in different periods. For example, he was once called Loden Chogsed, once Nyimai Ödzer, once Senge Dradog, and so on. For many centuries it was like this, because it is said that eight years after the parinirvana of Buddha Shakyamuni Guru Padmasambhava was born. It is said, however, that Padmasambhava was also the student of Shri

Simha, who lived many years after the Buddha. Although Tibetan historical texts believe that Guru Padmasambhava lived many thousands
of years, I am not really sure about that; for me it seems he had different
emanations at various times. The last one is the Guru Padmasambhava
who arrived in Tibet.

In any case, one of his emanations met and received transmissions
of Dzogchen teachings from Garab Dorje, and therefore we believe that
Guru Padmasambhava was not only a student of Shri Simha, but also of
Garab Dorje. From the time of Garab Dorje to Shri Simha, there were
many lineages and many intervening years.

When Guru Padmasambhava arrived in Tibet, he mainly transmitted Dzogchen Upadesha and the principal teachings of Dzogchen
Semde and Longde. Guru Padmasambhava gave advice to his student
Vairochana, who was very intelligent and could learn everything immediately and easily. He told Vairochana that he should learn Sanskrit, the
Oddiyana language, as well as many other languages. Vairochana went
to India and Oddiyana where he met Dzogchen teachers and found
original Dzogchen books that he translated into Tibetan.

VAIROCHANA

At the time of Guru Padmasambhava there were no Dzogchen tantras
in Tibet. There were only what in later times were considered Dzogchen
Upadesha *terma* teachings. It is thought that these were taught by Guru
Padmasambhava. As there was no Dzogchen Semde and Longde at this
time, Vairochana traveled with his friend to India and Oddiyana, where
they met Shri Simha. They studied with him and received teachings.
Finally, Vairochana returned to Tibet; and when he arrived there and
communicated Dzogchen Semde and Longde, he had some problems

with some teachers, particularly Indian teachers who were related to the Sutra system. These teachers considered that Vairochana was not correct; and as they had a very strong relationship with the Tibetan kings, they created some problems for Vairochana, who was then sent from central to eastern Tibet.

VIMALAMITRA

Then, later, a Tibetan king invited Vimalamitra, a very important Dzogchen teacher, to Tibet. When he arrived, he began giving Sutra teachings related to the gradual path. Vimalamitra wrote one book on *gomrim,* meditation based on the gradual path.

Vimalamitra was not really a gradual teacher. He was a Dzogchen teacher, but he was not able to communicate Dzogchen directly due to the great confusion during that period, when Sutra and Tantra teachings were more prevalent, and the Dzogchen teachings by Vairochana were not accepted. At that time Guru Padmasambhava was no longer in Tibet.

Vairochana had many problems, but later Vimalamitra arrived and first taught Sutra and then gradually communicated Dzogchen teachings. When Vimalamitra gave Dzogchen teachings, the Tibetan king really understood that they had been wrong. Vairochana was vindicated and asked to return. After returning to Central Tibet, he translated many books and taught and communicated Dzogchen teachings.

THE THREE STATEMENTS OF GARAB DORJE

The books Vairochana translated were mainly Dzogchen Semde and Longde. Dzogchen Semde, Longde, and Upadesha are the three Series of Dzogchen. Why are there three Series? All the Dzogchen teachings were taught by Garab Dorje during his life, after which he manifested the Rainbow Body. Mañjushrimitra received permission from Garab Dorje to collect all these teachings, one of which is the three statements of Garab Dorje:

1. Direct Introduction
2. Not Remaining in Doubt
3. Continuing in That State

He understood that these three statements of Garab Dorje really represent the essence of the Dzogchen teachings, and are also the guidelines of the Dzogchen teachings. For learning, teaching, and applying, all the teachings are related to these three statements. For that reason, he divided all Dzogchen tantras and *lungs* transmitted by Garab Dorje into these three Series. The Semde is related to the first statement, the Longde to the second statement, and the Upadesha to the last statement.

Regarding the teachings related to first statement, the Dzogchen Semde, *sem* means "mind" and *semnyid* means "nature of mind." In the word Semde, *de* means "series of teachings," but Semde doesn't mean "the series of teachings on mind." The word *sem* in Semde is the shortened version of *changchubsem,* in which *chang* means "purified," and *chub* means "perfected." Thus, *sem* means our "pure mind" or our "pure condition." In the real sense, in Sanskrit, we say *bodhichitta.*

BODHICHITTA IN SUTRA

"Bodhichitta" as used in the Sutra principle and in Dzogchen are not the same. In Sutra we consider two kinds of bodhichitta: absolute and relative. "Absolute bodhichitta" is realization of *shunyata*, or emptiness, and having that knowledge, while "relative bodhichitta" relates to cultivating compassion. In this case, absolute bodhichitta as used in the Sutra system is very close to bodhichitta as understood in Dzogchen.

There are two categories of relative bodhichitta. The first is the intention of doing something good in order to gain realization. The second is the actual application of engaging in action. Generally, these two are the most well known definitions of bodhichitta that are discussed. We don't speak much about absolute bodhichitta, which is considered something like the final goal of realization. What we need are these two relative bodhichittas—cultivating with intention, and application.

BODHICHITTA IN DZOGCHEN

In many original Dzogchen books, in the *lungs* or shortened tantras, or sometimes in a tantra itself, you cannot find mention of the word "Dzogchen." They always use the word *changchubsem*, "bodhichitta." We translate the bodhichitta of Dzogchen as "primordial state." If we look closely at the meaning of *changchubsem, chang* means "to purify," but in the Dzogchen teaching, our real nature is pure from the beginning; there is nothing to purify, as it is already purified. *Chub* means that everything is perfected from the beginning; there is no path upon which to progress, nor anything to develop. That quality of having a purified or perfected state is in our real nature of mind. That is bodhichitta, or *changchubsem.*

In the real sense, *changchubsem* means the same thing as Dzogchen. *Dzog* means "perfected in relation to all our qualities" and so on, and *chen* means "totally," "the totally perfected state." Thus, there is no difference if we say Dzogchen or *changchubsem.* We must not understand "bodhichitta" used in this context to refer to "relative bodhichitta." In the Dzogchen Semde tantras and *lungs,* they use the term "bodhichitta" hundreds of times, and it always refers in those contexts to the primordial state, our real nature.

DZOGCHEN SEMDE

Garab Dorje gave direct introduction to his students so that they could have knowledge through experience. The most diffused experience in Buddhist practice is emptiness, because that is taught and introduced in the Sutra teachings, and also practiced as Shine. Why? Because our nature is very confused, agitated, and charged. As all our tensions are agitated, we need to relax. When we are relaxing through fixation upon an object of meditation, for example, we can get into a calm state from which we can discover the state of emptiness. In the calm state, there is nothing but the nature of emptiness.

In emptiness we start to be able to distinguish thoughts, movements, and manifestations, and then we know how to go ahead with other experiences such as clarity. At the end we can have the experience of sensation, which is more concrete at the physical level. At first, however, we go with the experience of the calm state, the experience of emptiness.

In the Dzogchen Semde there are different methods of explaining the four contemplations: *nepa* (the calm state), *miyowa* (nonmovement), *nyamnyid* (equality), and *lhundrub* (self-perfection). At the end, there is also the state of integration. Sometimes there is only an explanation of being in a state of Shine and observing different kinds of experiences related to the five elements, without speaking of the four contemplations. There are different methods, not only one. Mainly, there are three very distinct methods in the Dzogchen Semde, but all are going primarily with the experience of emptiness and bringing one into the state of that knowledge. These are the characteristics of Dzogchen Semde.

All these kinds of teachings, which include tantras, *lungs*, and the advice and experience of teachers and Mahasiddhas like Garab Dorje, Shri Simha, and Jñanasutra, are referred to collectively as the Series of Dzogchen Semde, which is related to the first statement of Garab Dorje.

NOT REMAINING IN DOUBT

With the second statement of Garab Dorje—Not Remaining in Doubt—we not only learn in an intellectual way, but discover the meaning with experience. For example, we don't understand in an intellectual way how sugar tastes. If we have never had the experience of sugar, we don't know what "sweet" is. We can read many books introducing us to the meaning of "sweet," and we can learn and construct many ideas, but we can never have a concrete experience of "sweet" in this way.

If we get a small piece of chocolate and place it on our tongue, we can have a concrete experience. After that we have nothing to change. When people are following teachings you often hear things like, "Oh, I am a student of a Sakyapa, or a Gelugpa," or they consider themselves a student of someone. Then, when people follow the Dzogchen teachings they think, "Oh, I must change; I must become a student of Dzogchen; I am accepting this path; maybe I like this path; maybe it is more interesting than the Gelugpa teachings." You can have this kind of idea and maybe decide to change. You think there is something to change, and many people do.

When I arrived in India for the first time, for example, there was a French nun. She said she was originally Catholic, and then became

Theravadin and spent many years in Thailand. Later she arrived in India and became a student of a Kagyüdpa Lama. Then she said that she
didn't like some method, and that she became a student of a Nyingmapa Lama. During the period that I knew her, she wanted to become
a Sakyapa. Someone had told her I was Sakyapa because I spent many
years in a Sakyapa monastery, and my college was more in the Sakyapa
tradition. I knew the Sakyapa tradition and teachings very well. I had
received it all. She came to me and said she wanted to follow a Sakyapa
teacher. I told her, "I have no time, and don't know, really. I am not a
teacher, but only a student. And I am just visiting India. That's all."
Then she went away, and after two or three years someone told me she
became Hindu. I was very surprised.

Life is very short. Although there seem to be many different ways,
when we have this attitude it shows that we do not understand the teaching, and have never entered into any understanding. If we have really
entered into understanding, there is nothing to change. It doesn't mean
all the methods are the same; there are hundreds of different methods,
but the essence or substance of the teaching is the same. When we discover there is nothing to change, we don't have any problems. We meet
Sakyapas, Kagyüdpas, and Gelugpas; there is no problem; we are always
free. That means we have tasted sugar; we know the taste of sugar and
we are experts at that. We are no more dependent on only some information, so we no longer have any problems.

Similarly, Dzogchen Longde is related to not remaining in doubt.
That kind of teaching, the tantra *Longchen Rabjam Gyalpoi Gyüd*, the
Tantra of Infinite Space,[41] and, later, many other experiences of teachers,
is collectively called the Series of Dzogchen Longde. Both Dzogchen
Semde and Longde were brought from Oddiyana by Vairochana.

The way of applying Dzogchen Longde in the time of Vairochana and today is a little different. In the time of Vairochana, Dzogchen Longde was introduced, presented, and used in a more purely Dzogchen way. Later it developed as a mixture with Tantra.

Vairochana Teaches Longde

When Vairochana was invited from Gyalmo Tsawarong in eastern Tibet, close to China, back to Central Tibet, he met on the road along the way an eighty-five-year-old monk. The old monk was very interested in following Dzogchen teachings. He had heard the Dzogchen teachings of Vimalamitra and Vairochana. Although he had never met them, he had met a student of Vairochana called Yudra Nyingpo, who had given him some transmissions and had told the old monk that he needed to meet his teacher, Vairochana. When Vairochana returned, the old monk went to see him, and while he was very interested in the teachings, he also felt very upset, saying, "Now I am eighty-five years old, I am meeting you too late. I am sorry I can't follow, but can you give me some blessing so that I may meet this teaching in the next life?" He asked in that way.

Vairochana responded, "The Dzogchen teachings and knowledge do not depend on age and education." The monk then asked, "Then I can follow even though I am old?" Vairochana answered, "Of course!" Then Vairochana gave him a very condensed Longde teaching in Dzogchen style. He also gave him a meditation belt for sitting in a position, a meditation stick for controlling the body, and a *tsulshing* (a meditation stick with a bowl-shaped upper part to put beneath the chin). Generally, we don't use the *tsulshing*; we use it only when we do dark retreat. All of these helped the monk to do the positions for Longde—the *tsulshing*, the meditation stick, and the belt. So with these he was able to hold the positions for a long time.

In order to help the old man remember the principle of the Longde practice, Vairochana wrote some essential verses of the Longde on the inside and outside of the *tsulshing*. The old monk did this practice and gained realization in a short time. His lifespan was extended and his old age was not troubled. At the end of his life he manifested the Rainbow Body publicly. He was not a very great or famous teacher while he was living and had only a few students, but he became famous after he manifested the Rainbow Body. The only remains were his nails and hair, the sign of the Rainbow Body.

The disappearance of the body is something that exists also in Sutra realization, but particularly in the Dzogchen teachings through doing the practice of Tregchöd. If we apply emptiness and the practice of integration in a state of emptiness or some Tantric practice, there can also be a realization where the body disappears. That is called *lü dultren* in Tibetan; *lü* means "physical body," and *dultren* means "to enter the atom." This means slowly, slowly disappearing into emptiness; but that, however, is not the Rainbow Body.

THE RAINBOW BODY

The Rainbow Body means that our physical body disappears because it enters into its real nature of the five elements. Those five elements are the five colors. So even if the physical body is disappearing, the shape and everything are maintained as the five colors.

People have represented the idea of the Rainbow Body by painting *thangkas* of Guru Padmasambhava as a cluster of rainbow colors. That is not accurate. With the Rainbow Body the whole form remains—the nose, eyes, and so forth—but normal people cannot see it, because everything disappears into the elements. We cannot see it because we don't have the capacity to see the nature of the elements. If we are a little developed and have more clarity or realization, then we can see the Rainbow Body. In this case, the sign of the Rainbow Body is that the hair and nails remain, because these are impure aspects of the physical body. The physical body enters into a pure dimension, but what remains is that impure aspect.

Another way other than the ordinary Rainbow Body is the great transference of consciousness called *phowa chenpo*. According to some historical accounts, Garab Dorje manifested the Rainbow Body in that way. Other accounts say he manifested the ordinary Rainbow Body. In the biographies it is said that Vimalamitra and Guru Padmasambhava manifested the Great Transference, which means they did not even manifest death.

In the normal Rainbow Body they first manifest death, and afterwards they dissolve the physical body. For example, if you put a small piece of ice in the sunshine, the ice slowly becomes smaller and smaller as it is melting. In the same way, our physical material body melts into the nature of the elements, but its form remains. In this case, it is necessary to first manifest death, and then it takes a week, sometimes less, to manifest the Rainbow Body.

NYAGLA PEMA DÜDDUL

The teacher of my two teachers Changchub Dorje and Ayu Khandro,[42] Nyagla Pema Düddul, told his students, "Now I am dying. At the end of this month I will die, so come and we will spend it together." The students went there and did many days of Ganapuja for purifying the relationship between teacher and students, between student and student. If they had created some problem of *samaya*, they purified with the Ganapuja. He gave much advice, and in his book, *The Songs of Nyagla Pema Düddul,*[43] there is a record of the advice he gave to different students during that period.

Then, at the end, he said he wanted to go to the sacred mountain where he had discovered many *terma* teachings. He wanted to go there to die. Many students said, "Oh, please don't die. Remain; we need you." He said, "This is my time. When the time comes, everyone has to go; so I have to go. It is more important that you collaborate with me and follow the teaching." They went to the mountain and he asked them to put up his small tent, the same kind of tent that the practitioners of Chöd[44] use. He asked them to sew him inside because otherwise the mountain animals could enter. Then he asked them to go back to the Gar, the place where they resided, and do Guruyoga and other practices.

After returning, they did practice for seven days, and then they saw many rainbows and other interesting signs on the mountain. When they went back to the mountain, they opened the tent, and all they could see were the remains of hair and nails. Hundreds and hundreds of people came to see, and Nyagla Pema Düddul became very famous. Although when he was alive he had very few students, after his death everyone claimed to be his student.

OGYEN TENDZIN

One of my uncles, Ogyen Tendzin, who was a very good Dzogchen practitioner and a student of Adzom Drugpa,[45] and also one who practiced much Yantra Yoga, contemplation, and integration, realized the Rainbow Body. When I was very small, I spent some months in a retreat place, and I remember he was always sitting and doing meditation. I didn't understand much about what he was doing because I was very small, but I would try to get him to play with me because I was bored. Sometimes he would sit naked in the cave, and I would beat him and then run away.

Later, before I left Tibet, I went and spent some weeks with him with the particular purpose of learning Yantra Yoga well. I asked him many questions because there were many parts I didn't know well, or didn't remember. I also received some teachings. I received my first Dzogchen teachings from my uncle when I was seven years old. He gave me the whole series of Dzogchen Upadesha teachings from the *Longchen Nyingthig*.[46]

He also manifested the Rainbow Body at the time of the Cultural Revolution. He was living in Yidlhung, in Derge (east Tibet), at the house of a very famous noble family, where he remained until the end of his life.

In this family there was a man, also a Dzogchen practitioner, and a student of my uncle, who rose very high in a Chinese office. My uncle was living on the roof of their very big palace, always doing retreat. As this man was my uncle's student, he was doing service for him. My uncle lived there for many years, and was living there during the Cultural Revolution. When at one point the revolutionaries seized him, some Tibetan functionaries of the Chinese office who had faith in my uncle found a way to secure his freedom.

Once my uncle was free, he didn't know where to go or where to live, and so the official said he would find him a place where the nomads stay in the winter. There was a small house, and my uncle lived there. That functionary went every weekend to visit him, bring a little food, and check up on him.

One day he and another Chinese official knocked on the door and it didn't open. They thought maybe my uncle had fled. Knocking down the door, they saw his robe on the bed; but as he was apparently not there, they looked inside the robe and found a small body inside. They knew that Ogyen Tendzin was no longer alive, but had become a small body. They shut the door and went away. We didn't find out what had happened after my uncle died until 1978. Then we received news from Derge that after two or three days, some Chinese functionaries had reported that Togden had died, and had left only hair and nails. The Rainbow Body still exists even today—it is not only something from ancient times.

In Dzogchen Longde many teachers have manifested the Rainbow Body. In later times, Dzogchen practitioners were mostly doing practice of Dzogchen Upadesha; Longde remained only a transmission. For example, when I received transmission of Dzogchen Semde and Longde, there was only the lineage of transmission, but no one was doing the actual practice of Longde or Dzogchen Semde. It had disappeared. Everybody had become engaged with Dzogchen Upadesha.

In ancient times, Vimalamitra manifested the Great Transference, and his student Nyang Tingdzin Zangpo manifested the Rainbow Body. However, after Nyang Tingdzin Zangpo, the realization of the Rainbow Body did not occur for four or five generations. Although we do not know very precisely, it seems there had been some problems in the transmission.

CHETSÜN SENGE WANGCHUG

Then there was a teacher called Chetsün Senge Wangchug (eleventh-twelfth century), a great *tertön* who discovered a Dzogchen Upadesha *terma* teaching.[47] He met Vimalamitra in the Rainbow Body and spent three months with him. Vimalamitra transmitted all the Dzogchen Upadesha transmissions, and particularly Dzogchen Upadesha tantras. People considered that Chetsün Senge Wangchug had some special transmissions because later on he manifested the Rainbow Body.

After Chetsün Senge Wangchug, the lineage was restored, and many teachers in the Dzogchen Upadesha lineage manifested the Rainbow Body. This is the reason why all later Dzogchen practitioners were doing Dzogchen Upadesha, while Dzogchen Semde and Longde remained on the periphery. The transmission, however, is still alive and has never been interrupted.

11   Terma Teachings—Refreshing the Transmission[48]

When you receive a teaching of any kind, especially if it is linked to Tantra or Dzogchen, you have to know the source of that teaching and its connection to the lineage of transmission. A teaching has its origin and its principle, so you can understand that it is not something invented by somebody. If someone invented it with their intellect, it could not work. A teaching must have been taught and transmitted by a being who was totally realized, such as Buddha Shakyamuni, Garab Dorje, or Vajrasattva.

There is always the source of a teaching, and a continuous uninterrupted lineage from that source to the master from whom you receive that teaching. It is very important for you to understand the lineage and source of the teaching. If one day you have to transmit this teaching, you have to know where it comes from. So whenever I give a teaching, I always try to make you understand what the source of that teaching is.

PURE VISION

We can also have transmission through *tagnang*, pure vision. If we are good practitioners of Dzogchen Longde, Thödgal, or Yangti,[49] then we can develop pure vision, through which Guru Padmasambhava, Garab Dorje, and other masters can manifest, and we can receive teachings and clarifications. The reason is that we have already received and connected with the transmission that is alive in us, and through which we can have a relationship with those masters. Having that kind of transmission of the teaching is called *tagnang*.

The same is true for many of the teachings of Namchö Mingyur Dorje (1645-1667). *Namchö* is the name given to the teachings of Mingyur Dorje. *Nam* means "space"; *chö* means "teaching"; so together it means "the teachings of space." What does that mean? It means that visions such as the Sambhogakaya and so forth manifested in space, and that he received transmission through those manifestations.

The practice of the Shitro from this cycle of teachings is an example of this kind of transmission. At the end of the Shitro practice it says that when Mingyur Dorje was twelve years old Vajrasattva appeared in his vision one day while he was sitting and communicated that teaching to him. He immediately dictated it to his disciples, who then wrote it down. So *namchö* means "a teaching coming from space," but in fact it does not come from space, but from the manifestation of Vajrasattva. *Tagnang* is the name usually given to these types of teachings.

Another very interesting aspect of *tagnang*, and a famous example of *tagnang* Dzogchen teachings, are those visions that came to the first Düdjom Rinpoche. The Düdjom Rinpoche who recently passed away was a reincarnation of the *tertön* Düdjom Lingpa (1835-1903). When the first *tertön* Düdjom Lingpa was in contemplation of the Thödgal, a practice through which one can have many visions, there appeared in his vision a *thigle,* or sphere, in which there was a manifestation of Guru Tsokye Dorje, or Guru Padmasambhava in Sambhogakaya form, who communicated a teaching to him. Remaining in a state of contemplation, Düdjom Lingpa received this communication, and then repeated all the teachings he was receiving to two disciples who were by his side and wrote them down.

This comprises a very thick volume of pure Dzogchen teaching that is very interesting. If we read it, we can see that it was not something that was composed intellectually. This teaching is called *tagnang yeshe trawa. Tagnang* means that it is a teaching that has come through pure vision; *yeshe* means "wisdom"; *trawa* means "a net," or "a manifestation through light." That is an example of *tagnang,* and there are many of these kinds of teachings.

DREAMS

Another aspect of *tagnang* can come through dreams, and there are many masters who have had this type of teaching. For example, I received through my dreams both the Dance of the Vajra[50] and the form of the mandala on which it is danced. They are not something that didn't exist before, and certainly the principle of the Dance of the Vajra and the Song of the Vajra existed in the Dzogchen tantras, although there was not a Dance of the Vajra danced on a mandala, or the precise form of the mandala. These were all things I received in my dreams, not only through the dream of a single night, but through the dreams of many months. I wrote down all the teachings I received in these dreams. You can see that there are many types of teachings, and many of the teachings called *terma* arise from the clarity of one's mind.

MIND TREASURE

There is another aspect of the transmission generally called *gongter*. *Gong* is the state of the mind; *ter* is a treasure that is put in the mind and which then appears. We have many interesting *gongter* teachings. An example from the Dzogchen Upadesha is a series of teachings called the *Khandro Nyingthig*, which means "Essential Teachings of the Dakinis." This teaching was given by Guru Padmasambhava, who made it into a *terma* in order to keep the teachings and transmission pure for the future. He put this *ter* into the mind of the daughter of the Tibetan king Trisong Deutsen. This daughter was very young and was dying. In fact, in the stories it is said that she was already dead. The king was suffering terribly and asked, "Why do I have to suffer so much? This is my daughter who is so young, and she has already died."

Guru Padmasambhava told him a story. In very ancient times he and Shantarakshita and the king were all at work building the very big *chörten* (Skt. *stupa*) at Boudhanath in Kathmandu, Nepal. One day, while building this *chörten,* King Trisong Deutsen squashed a mosquito that had stung him. While the mosquito was stinging him, the king slapped the point where it was stinging and accidentally killed it without intending to. He had interrupted that life and so had created a negative action. There had been a very precise connection between that mosquito and Trisong Deutsen, and as a repayment of the debt in that life this mosquito had become his daughter. She did not, however, have the positive karma to live a long life in order for them to have contact with each other. This is the way Guru

Padmasambhava explained it so that the king would understand and not suffer so much.

Then the king asked Guru Padmasambhava, "Please do something. What can we do to have some benefit?" Guru Padmasambhava said, "You do not have to worry, because although your daughter is very young, she has already received a very important transmission of the teaching that will greatly benefit her realization." To make the king happy, and for the benefit of the future, Guru Padmasambhava summoned back the consciousness of the dead daughter into her corpse, gave her the specific introduction, and put the *terma* of the *Khandro Nyingthig* into her mind.

After many lives that daughter was reborn as the *tertön* Pema Ledrel Tsal (1291-1315), who, even when he was very young, had many capacities. All these teachings of the *Khandro Nyingthig* came through him, and he wrote them down and transmitted them. The Third Karmapa, Rangjung Dorje (1284-1339), was very interested, received them, and became a holder of this lineage.

Before Pema Ledrel Tsal managed to write down all these teachings, he died. There is also a very precise reason why that happened. His immediate reincarnation was Longchenpa, who, when he was young, started proclaiming that he was Pema Ledrel Tsal. He studied and became a very famous scholar, and to complete the series of teachings of Pema Ledrel Tsal he wrote the *Khandro Yangtig*, one of four Upadesha series of teachings included in the *Nyingthig Yazhi*.[51]

These teachings are usually called mind *terma*, of which there are many types. When there is this kind of *terma*, then the lineage of the transmission is called direct. There is never, however, the continuity of the direct lineage without also the official line of transmission. These must always be tied and connected together, because we live in the limited human condition. For example, when we pursue an intellectual study such as history we always have to have some reference as proof. In the same way, it is not enough to say that this is a mind *terma* of somebody, and that is its history. It is possible to clarify some things, but it has to have its foundation, its history related to social conditions, and to the teaching.

While the *kama*[52] teaching is very important, *termas* have to adorn and enrich this knowledge and above all, refresh the transmission. Sometimes in the *kama* transmission there can be some problems because within the lineage the transmission from master to disciple has to be very pure. If it is not pure, and some problem is created, it becomes an obstacle to the functioning of the transmission. That is where it has to be connected with the *terma* transmission.

12   Yantra Yoga[53]

The word *yantra* is a Sanskrit word, but in Tibetan it has different meanings. It can refer to a geometrical form such as a mandala. In Tibetan, *yantra* can also mean "movement of the body." The group of forms with movement is referred to as Yantra Yoga. In Tibetan we say *trulkhor,* "movement," which we use for coordinating or guiding our prana, or vital energy. There are different kinds of Yantras associated with the various Anuttaratantras, such as the Yantras related to the Hevajra Tantra, the Yantras related to the Kalachakra Tantra, and similarly with other tantras.

YANTRA YOGA LINEAGE

That which I teach is called Yantra Yoga, or *Nyida Khajor.* In Tibetan, *nyida* means "sun and moon," and *khajor* means "union." That is the title of the original teaching, which was taught by a very famous Tibetan teacher called Vairochana, one of the most important students of Guru Padmasambhava. During the time of the Tibetan king Trisong Deutsen, Guru Padmasambhava was invited to Tibet, where

he introduced Vajrayana. At that time there was this famous transla-
tor called Vairochana, who was a very important figure, particularly
for the Dzogchen teaching, because he translated most of the original
Dzogchen texts from the language of Oddiyana into Tibetan. He received the transmission of the Yantra Yoga teaching from Guru Padmasambhava, who had received it from Mahasiddha Humkara. This
is the lineage of the teaching that comes from Vairochana, who taught
it to his students such as Yudra Nyingpo, among others. Thus we have
this transmission and the continuation of this very ancient tradition of
Yantra.

ORAL TRANSMISSION

Besides Vairochana's text, there is also an oral transmission of Yantra
Yoga. It is very difficult to understand Yantra Yoga if you only read the
original text of Vairochana and do not have a teacher. Practitioners
of Dzogchen particularly have applied these methods for centuries.
I learned them principally from one of my uncles, who was a yogi
and an excellent practitioner of Yantra. After I had been in Italy for
several years, many people became interested in Tantric teachings
and Yoga. Gradually it was necessary for me to teach this method
of Yantra to those who were interested. I had made many notes when
I had studied, and then later I wrote a book, a commentary on Vairochana's text.

We call this book *Yantra Yoga*, but its title is *Nyida Khajor;* and even
though the title of this book is *Nyida Khajor*, Vairochana himself men-
tions the term *Yantra* at the end of the text, which is why we generally
use the name Yantra Yoga.[54]

Our Real Condition

We find the word *yoga* in the Sanskrit language, but when we use "Yoga" in Tibetan, we translate it as *naljor,* which has a very precise meaning. While we usually define the meaning of "Yoga" as "union," when we say *naljor* in Tibetan, it means "primordial knowledge or understanding." *Nal* means "original," "authentic," or "unchanging"—"the original condition"; *jor* means "having" or "discovering" this knowledge or understanding. Thus, the real meaning of "Yoga" is that we discover our real condition.

In the practice of Yantra Yoga, we use our body, speech, and mind. With the body there are positions and movements; with the voice there are many different techniques of *pranayama,* or breathing practices, and with the mind there are many ways to concentrate and visualize. The aim of these methods is to go beyond judging and thinking into the state of contemplation. This is how our three existences of body, speech, and mind are related, and when we apply all three together, we have the possibility of arriving at real knowledge, and the understanding of our original condition. This is really the meaning of "Yoga" in Yantra Yoga.

Breathing and Movement

In Yantra Yoga there are many positions similar to those of Hatha Yoga, but the way of getting into the positions, the main point of the practice, and the consideration or point of view of the practice of Yantra Yoga are different. In Yantra Yoga, the asana, or position, is an important point, but is not the main one. Movement is more important. For example, in order to get into an asana, breathing and movement are linked and applied gradually. Each movement is divided into periods of time consisting of four beats each: a period to enter the position, a period to remain in the position, and then a period to complete the position. As everything is related in Yantra Yoga, the overall movement is important, not only the asana.

UNDERSTANDING ENERGY

The system of Yantra Yoga that we apply is from a book written by Vairochana in which 108 movements are described related to different types of breathing. When we consider the three aspects of body, speech, and mind, which of them is more important? While the mind is more important, it is easier to understand through the body because our body is related to the material level. We can see, we can touch, we can have a very concrete understanding through the physical body. If, however, we want to have a deeper understanding on the level of energy, then the situation is more complicated.

In the same way, if we ask which is more important in Yantra Yoga, the movement or the prana energy, of course the latter is more important, as well as the way we coordinate it and use it through breathing related to visualization. If we have a physical problem, how can we guide the prana energy? We do this through breathing related to visualization or concentration. When there are physical problems or disorders associated with the five elements, we concentrate on the characteristic color, seed syllable, or the sound of the seed syllable related to the particular element; and using sound and visualization, we can guide the prana and coordinate our energy. This is the reason teachers of Yoga are always demonstrating methods for overcoming problems related to energy disorders in our body. Although the energy level is more important than the physical, even more essential is the mind, which in Yoga is considered like a king, while the energy is like the government, and the physical body like the subjects of the country. Everything is governed in this way.

Physical positions and movements are, however, also very important, because if we are not able to control our physical level, there is no way we can control our energy. If we cannot control our energy, then there is no way we can control our mind. Mind is dependent on energy, which in turn depends on the physical body. In Yantra Yoga these three aspects become balanced by working firstly on the physical level with positions and movements that are a means for coordinating or harmonizing our energy.

In the Yantra Yoga of Vairochana there are seventy-five different positions or movements that are divided into five groups. In these five groups, there are five different techniques of breathing, or *pranayama*, to control prana energy. Why do we need to control this function of energy, or prana? That is the only way in which we can really become aware and enter into the real condition of mind.

When we consider mind and the nature of mind, the nature of mind means its potentiality, which we can govern. If we govern the potentiality of the nature of mind, that means that we are on the path and that we have the possibility for realization. If we are ignorant of that, then we become a slave to mind and judgment. In this case we need to coordinate our physical body and our energy. For this reason Vairochana gave this Yantra Yoga teaching, which is a characteristic teaching of Dzogchen.

Transformation

The principal methods of Dzogchen are a little different from the methods of the Tantric teaching of Anuttaratantra, or Highest Yoga Tantra. For example, when we talk about Tantric teaching, the characteristic method is transformation, while in the Sutra teaching it is the path of renunciation, in which we renounce the cause of negativities and control our existence. If, for example, we consider emotions, in the Sutra teachings they are called "poisons." Being conditioned by them, we can have many problems and create a lot of negative potentiality; however, in the teachings of Anuttaratantra, even if they are "poisons," they can be transformed. The emotions are not considered to be without value, because they are related to our energy. The real meaning of the nature of the emotions is energy, which is an aspect of our real condition. For that reason there is a possibility to transform them.

Self-Liberation

Atiyoga, or the Dzogchen teaching, is found particularly in the Nyingmapa tradition. *Ati* means "primordial state" in the language of Oddiyana; *yoga* means "knowledge" or "understanding." This is a characteristic of the Dzogchen teaching, and this method is not transformation, but self-liberation. The Yantra Yoga of Vairochana belongs to the Atiyoga system of the Dzogchen teaching, and for that reason has no particular visualization of deities or transformation. If you learn other kinds of Yantra Yoga, such as that of Hevajra, Vajravarahi, or Kalachakra, then first of all you must receive the initiation of the tantra, and then practice the development and the accomplishing stages in order to practice Yantra Yoga and work with prana energy.

However, since the Yantra Yoga of Vairochana belongs to the system of Atiyoga, we do not always use practices of transformation such as visualization of deities and so on. When we visualize channels and chakras and so forth, we always start with what is called *tongra*; *tong* means "emptiness," and *ra* means "dimension." The dimension of emptiness means that we do not transform ourselves, but remain present in the knowledge of emptiness. We have our dimension, and our dimension is emptiness.

PREPARATORY MOVEMENTS

As was stated before, the Vairochana system of Yantra Yoga consists of five different types of prana practices and many different movements which are each linked to time: a period of time for getting into a position, a period for remaining in it, and another for finishing the position. This is a very precise system characteristic of this Yantra Yoga. Before we do these five types of breathing and their corresponding movements, there are important preparatory practices.

When we learn how to do a practice of prana energy from a teacher, there is no guarantee that we will understand how to apply it correctly. In Yantra Yoga first of all there are eight movements related to the eight characteristic ways of breathing: exhaling, inhaling, slowly or quickly, holding closed or open, and so on. If we learn these eight movements and apply them sufficiently, we will surely succeed when the teacher explains how to do the breathing in a prana practice, because we know how to apply the breathing correctly through having practiced the eight movements.

After this, there are two different series of five movements for co-ordinating our energy in a precise way. These eighteen movements, one series of eight, and two of five, are considered preliminary practices. Then we go on to the main movements and positions.

BREATHING

When we learn the first group of movements we apply one type of breathing in a very precise way. There are five of these groups, each with a different type of breathing or prana practice related to characteristic methods that are believed to have different effects. Some are more related to coordinating energy, some are related to developing the *kumbhaka* holding. The purpose of these practices is mainly for coordinating our breathing in daily life.

In general, everyone knows how to inhale and exhale, but we usually do this in an incorrect way because our breathing is linked to our mind, which is often disordered and confused. We can understand this when we observe the breathing of a person who is very agitated, or of someone who is very quiet and peaceful. For this reason it is necessary to coordinate our breathing. In Yoga we say that life is breathing, and it is true, because we started our life when we started to breathe. Cessation of breath means cessation of life. When we exhale and do not inhale again then there is no more life.

The Tantric teaching explains how many breaths a person uses in one day. A person who practices Yantra Yoga is said to have a long life because their breathing is coordinated. How can we coordinate it? One of the most important methods is by practicing *kumbhaka*. If we have capacity for *kumbhaka* holding and practice frequently, it will influence our daily lives so that our breathing, instead of being dominated by thoughts and judgment, will become more coordinated.

SENSATION

There are also practices such as that of inner heat, or what is called *tummo* in Tibetan. It means that one is not affected by cold. We can develop inner heat through the capacity of coordinating prana, and with one of the five types of breathing used in Yantra Yoga. The reason for the practice of inner heat is precisely because heat is the basis for sensation. In Tantra we say that we need to develop heat in order to develop sensation, and we need to develop sensation if we want to deepen our knowledge and our understanding of the final goal of the state of contemplation.

The final goal of Anuttaratantra is the state of Mahamudra, or "total symbol," which refers to the deity, the mandala, the visualization, and transformation—everything as a symbolic totality. Mahamudra is the symbol through which our existence of body, voice, and mind are completely integrated. We integrate through different experiences such as those of clarity and emptiness, but mainly through the experience of the sensation of pleasure. All these are considered important methods for having knowledge. Similarly, in the Dzogchen teaching, we apply practices such as Tummo to develop our capacity for sensation and other experiences.

13 The Three Sacred Principles[55]

The Three Sacred Principles are three fundamental aspects of the teaching that are always explained right from the beginning. This is true not only in the Dzogchen teachings, but also at the level of Sutra and Tantra. The first of these Three Sacred Principles is Refuge and Bodhichitta; the second is Contemplation; and the third is Dedication of Merit.

At a practical level, what the first and the third of these three principles mean is that when we start a practice, we begin it with an idea or thought; and similarly, when we finish a practice and return to our normal activities again, we begin those activities guiding ourselves with an idea or thought. The fact is that we are not always in the state of contemplation. Even if we have some experience or knowledge of this state, most of the time we are distracted from it. In order to find ourselves in the state of contemplation, we start by guiding ourselves towards it with a particular thought.

Let's assume, for example, that we have at least intellectually understood that our real nature is like that of a mirror that has the capacity to reflect everything without judging it to be good or bad, without accepting or rejecting anything. How can we, on the basis of our intellectual understanding, actually discover this real nature in ourselves? How can we enter into the true state of knowledge and thus come to a real experience of how our thoughts and emotions are actually like reflections in a mirror? We begin by guiding ourselves with the thought of wishing to attain enlightenment for the benefit of all sentient beings. We do this with the Refuge and Bodhichitta.

REFUGE AND BODHICHITTA

It is important, particularly in Dzogchen, to understand what Refuge and Bodhichitta really mean, how to apply them practically, and not just remain at the level of words and external forms.

The origins of the practices of Refuge and Bodhichitta are to be found in the Sutra system. In both the Hinayana and Mahayana systems of Sutra, the way in which one takes refuge determines whether an individual is considered to be Buddhist or not. In Sutra, if a person takes refuge in the Buddha, Dharma, and Sangha, such a person is considered to be a Buddhist. I have personally been criticized by some people who claim that I am not a Buddhist because I use another form of Refuge—taking refuge in the Guru, Deva, and Dakini instead of taking refuge in the Buddha, Dharma, and Sangha.

Such criticism is based on a fundamental misunderstanding of the principle involved, because "Guru, Deva, and Dakini" do not mean something different from "Buddha, Dharma, and Sangha." The principle of the teachings does not depend on the superficial level of the names by which things are called, but on the real sense and meaning behind those names. We must understand what "Guru, Deva, and Dakini" mean. These are terms used in the Tantric system.

Generally speaking, when we use the word "Buddhist," what we are referring to is someone who follows the teaching of the Buddha himself, or something related to the teaching of the Buddha himself. At least this is what is meant by the term Buddhist in the Hinayana view. The official Buddhist teaching is considered in that tradition to be only that knowledge and understanding that the physical Buddha himself actually transmitted. There are, however, many other teachings the Buddha transmitted in manifestations other than his physical body. This is the origin of Tantric transmission. How did the Buddha manifest to transmit the tantras? To transmit these teachings he did not manifest in the form of Buddha Shakyamuni—the physical, historical Buddha—but rather in different ways according to circumstances, and not just according to someone's rule. For a Buddha, there is no rule that his form must be a figure like that of the historical Buddha Shakyamuni. The form he manifests depends upon circumstances, and a Buddha will work with the situation in which he finds himself.

A Buddha will sometimes manifest in a form similar to those beings to whom he is trying to communicate knowledge and understanding. When a Buddha communicates to an elephant or a monkey, for example, he may manifest as that kind of being. He can do this because he is free. He is able to work with any circumstances; he never remains limited by rules. People who are limited do not understand this and they believe a Buddha can only manifest on the physical level. They believe that if the physical form of the Buddha is not the one with which they are familiar, then this form is not a Buddha at all.

The manifestations of Deva and Dakini are none other than the Buddha, who can manifest in many different ways, not only in the form of a human being. There is a saying in the sutras that the Buddha sometimes manifests as a bridge or as a boat in order to save people; it is not necessary that he should always manifest as a human being. There are many possibilities of manifestation. This is the principle of Deva and Dakini.

Similarly, Refuge is not limited to the taking of a vow as it is in the Hinayana view. Many people like to say that they have taken Refuge with this or that Lama. There are teachers who travel widely and give Refuge vows everywhere, claiming that they have converted enormous numbers of people to Buddhism. They seem to think of Refuge as if it were a matter of conquering people.

This is not how the teachings should be spread. Spreading the teachings really means helping people to wake up and understand something; it should not become another means of conditioning people. That is not to say, of course, that it is not useful for people to take a vow of Refuge if they understand its real sense and meaning. When they do not, however, understand its meaning, they can deceive themselves into believing that something has changed in them when it has not. If they really honestly observe themselves, they will see that their conditioning, attachments, and problems are all still there and are just the same as before they took the vow. Nothing has changed. What then is the benefit of taking refuge? The real point is to know and understand what Refuge means.

Vows

Refuge can be taken with a vow. If we don't have the capacity to control ourselves, we need to take a vow. The Hinayana specifically aims to help individuals whose capacity to integrate emotions is less developed. Taking a vow, such people are able to control their emotions and problems and avoid creating negative karma.

We should not think that since we are Dzogchen practitioners, we are particularly highly developed and do not need vows. Many people have this idea, but it is not true. We must observe ourselves well. We have many weak points. When people want to stop smoking or drinking, for example, they may not succeed for a long time because it is their weak point. Sometimes it is necessary to take a vow to deal with a situation like this. There are people who are not in the Dzogchen Community who have told me that my students are very arrogant, that they feel themselves to be at a very high level and do not feel the need to do the *ngöndro*, or preliminary practices, that are commonly done.

To think that just because we are Dzogchen practitioners we do not need a vow is completely wrong. When we discover we have a weak point, we may need a vow to help us overcome it. This is why it is said in Dzogchen that we should work with our circumstances. What do we mean by this? Even if we understand that, at the absolute level, spontaneous self-perfection is our inherent condition, and that rules and vows are not necessary at that level, if in our own particular circumstances we find that there are problems we cannot overcome without such methods, then we apply a rule or a vow. The difference between Dzogchen and other levels of teaching is that these relative methods of rules and vows are not considered to be the main point. They are not the fundamental method of Dzogchen practice as they are in Sutra.

In the Hinayana, for example, receiving a vow is considered to be the single most important aspect of the training. In Dzogchen we proceed differently, and although a vow might be used if necessary, it is not the principal method. Of course, if it's the case that someone has received the Refuge vow from a teacher other than myself, then they need to understand its meaning and function. It is ridiculous to think that just because we have taken a Refuge vow we have become Buddhist. It does not mean anything to say we are Buddhist on that basis. The

Buddha never asked anyone to become a Buddhist, nor did the Buddha ever propose these limitations. These are our own limitations projected onto the teachings.

THE REAL MEANING OF REFUGE

Therefore, we must try to understand the real sense of the teaching. The real meaning of Refuge is to know that we are on the path. We take refuge in the path. How do we find that path? We find it from a teacher. If there is no teacher, there is no path. Whether we speak of Sutra, Tantra, or Dzogchen, the root of the path is always the teacher.

When we take refuge in the Sutra system, with the first words we recite, "Namo Buddhaya," we take refuge in the Buddha; then we take refuge in the Dharma, and in the Sangha. In Tantra, the way of seeing Buddha and the way of seeing the teacher, or Guru, is a little different. In Sutra, the Buddha is understood to be the origin of the teaching, the source of the path. The final goal is seen as the state of the Buddha, or the Dharmakaya. For this reason we take refuge in the Buddha at this level of the teaching.

In Tantra and Dzogchen, we take refuge principally in the Guru. This is because, even though it is the teachings of the Buddha that we are following, we have received them from our own teacher. We can never receive teachings directly from the Buddha. Although we do not even have direct contact with the Buddha's direct students, his students taught other disciples and so on, and in this way the teachings have continued until the present day, when our teacher taught them to us.

Tantra is also particularly related to special transmissions such as empowerments. In Dzogchen the principle is to give direct introduction to the state of knowledge and understanding. The students receive this transmission of the introduction from their teacher. Although we may receive explanations or methods that have originated from the Buddha, we can only receive direct transmissions from our own teacher. We can never receive such transmissions from the Buddha. As our teacher is extremely important for us, and because the teacher is the source from which something originated, he or she is referred to as the "root Guru." Our root Guru is the source of all transmissions, knowledge, and understanding, and therefore, when we take refuge in the context of Tantra or Dzogchen, we first take refuge in the Guru.

In Dzogchen particularly, when we take refuge, we do so in the Guru. This means that the teacher is considered more important than other persons. If there is a Guru, there is a teaching. This is the principle of transmission.

SANGHA

When we speak of the Sangha, we are referring to people with whom we collaborate on the path. In Dzogchen, Sangha can also refer to the Dharmapalas, or "Guardians," beings who help us on our path to realization.

In the Sutra system, when we speak in terms of Buddha, Dharma, and Sangha, the teacher is considered to be part of the Sangha. What does Sangha mean? In Sutra, Sangha refers to a group of at least four monks. For example, if an individual wants to receive the full vow of a monk or nun, he or she receives it from a Sangha of at least four monks. Three monks is not enough. One cannot receive the full vow just from the teacher. A Refuge vow can be taken from the teacher, but the complete vows of monk or nun can only be received from the Sangha.

Similarly, in the Sutra system, if we make a mistake, we confess it to the Sangha. We cannot confess to the teacher. It is characteristic of the Sutra level that in order to make a confession we always need a Sangha. For this reason, the teacher is part of the Sangha, and the Sangha is considered to be the group of people that helps us.

In Dzogchen, on the other hand, the teacher is indispensable. In the Sutra system, if there is no teacher, we nevertheless still have the teachings of the Buddha. As long as we have the possibility of learning words, reading books, or studying with a group of people, we can still go ahead. That is not possible in Tantra and in Dzogchen. If we want to follow the Dzogchen teachings, we must receive an introduction from a teacher, otherwise our knowledge is not connected with the transmission, and there can be no enlightenment. Similarly, in Tantra, it is necessary to receive an empowerment from a teacher. Otherwise, even if we know many Tantric methods, our situation remains like a plowed field in which no seeds have ever been sown; even if we work it for years and years, nothing will grow in such a field.

Whether or not we take a vow of Refuge does not matter, but we must understand the meaning of Refuge, because Refuge and Bodhichitta together are the first of the Three Sacred Principles.

BODHICHITTA

Bodhichitta is a term found principally in the Mahayana, which speaks a great deal about the two truths, absolute and relative. By "absolute truth" we mean our real condition, the condition of things as they truly are. When we do not have knowledge of this real condition, we remain conditioned by the relative dimension, and that is what is called the "relative truth." In the Sutra teaching, relative truth is considered to be like samsara, the state of confused, deluded mind; and absolute truth is considered to be like knowledge, or understanding, or the state of nirvana. The terms "nirvana" and "samsara" correspond respectively to absolute truth and relative truth.

Bodhichitta is also explained in that way, in terms of absolute and relative. Absolute bodhichitta means having real experiential knowledge of emptiness, which arises through practice. It is not just having an intellectual idea of emptiness. In the Sutra teaching, one of the principal practices is Shine, developing a calm state through which we discover emptiness.

When we have experience of emptiness and our knowledge has become more concrete, then finally we can consider that we have at least a little experience of absolute bodhichitta. Absolute bodhichitta is the experience of emptiness from which its compassionate energy or function manifests.

COMPASSION

When we speak of bodhichitta in general, what we are speaking of is compassion. What is compassion? Compassion arises through our feeling as an experience we have in relation to others. Where does it arise? Compassion arises from emptiness, which is its source and its basis. In an empty sky, for example, you can't find anything; however, sometimes clouds appear in an empty sky. They arise, they develop, and they disappear again into an empty sky. The same is also true of bodhichitta, or compassion. Compassion also manifests from emptiness.

That is the reason why, when we are speaking of Tantra, we always speak of emptiness and clarity. Emptiness and clarity are functions of the same principle. All manifestation comes from emptiness, which is represented as the sky. When we speak of the Dharmadhatu, *dharma* means "all phenomena," and *dhatu* means "the real condition of emptiness." Although there is total emptiness, from that emptiness everything manifests. When we speak of the manifestation of the five elements, the first of these is the element of space from which everything manifests. The element of space is emptiness. If there were no element of space, there would be no possibility of manifestation.

In the same way, compassion manifests from emptiness, the real knowledge of which is called absolute bodhichitta. Relative bodhichitta, which is compassion, is related to our thoughts, our sensations, our feelings, and to everything that develops in the dimension of samsara. Sometimes, even when we do have compassion, it is still something limited. For that reason, in our training we practice cultivating compassion beyond our limitations. Otherwise, our compassion and love might always remain limited. For example, a mother has compassion and love for her children; but she never loves anyone else the way she loves her children. In the same way, when people fall in love they are at that moment conditioned by their emotions, and never love anyone else in the same way. That is what we mean when we speak of our compassion being limited.

When we cultivate bodhichitta, it means going beyond limitations characteristic of our dualistic vision. From the beginning we have our narrow ego, our sense of "I," and even if we expand our thinking a little and speak of "ourselves"—where at first we said "I," and now we are saying "we," and developing things along those lines—we nevertheless always remain within defined limits. Through the teaching and developing real knowledge we can go beyond that. Working with our intention and thinking, we cultivate bodhichitta. Diminishing our attachment to ego, we place others before ourselves in order to benefit them. The bodhichitta principle is a fundamental teaching of the Mahayana. If we ask, "Why do we follow Mahayana teachings? What do we practice in the Mahayana?," the answer is very simple: we observe our intention and try to cultivate a good intention in everything we do. That is the total practice of Mahayana.

TRANSMISSION

Following the teachings of Tantra or Dzogchen always involves the principle of transmission, which is not something we can receive through reading books, or only through the words of an oral explanation. That kind of approach is more characteristic of how we might follow the Sutra teachings.

In Dzogchen, transmission is the life of the teaching; we cannot attain realization without it. There are three kinds of transmission; direct, oral, and symbolic. Garab Dorje was the first human teacher of Dzogchen on this planet in this time cycle. Before he concluded his life with the realization of the Rainbow Body, he summarized his teaching in what became known as the Three Statements of Garab Dorje. The first of these statements is "Direct Introduction." In this direct introduction, the teacher introduces the student to the state of contemplation through experiences of body, voice, and mind.

The second statement is "Not Remaining in Doubt." The student experiences the state of contemplation through the transmission he or she has received in the direct introduction, and no longer has any doubt as to what contemplation is.

The third statement is "Continuing in the State." This means that the student seeks to remain in the state of contemplation all the time, remaining in the natural condition of instant presence without correcting it, and applying practices as necessary according to circumstances to reenter the state when she or he has become distracted from it.

Thus, when we practice Guruyoga, what we are trying to do is to discover the state in which the teacher continually abides and has transmitted to us. When we are in the state of contemplation, there is no separation between the teacher and ourselves. Through Guruyoga we can enter the state of contemplation. In Dzogchen the teacher is indispensable, because without receiving direct transmission from the teacher, there can be no realization.

Along with this method of direct introduction I have just explained, there are in fact two other kinds of transmission mentioned in the Dzogchen teachings. "Oral Transmission" refers to general explanations of the teachings, or to particular instructions relating to various methods, such as instructions for visualizations.

"Symbolic Transmission" refers to the use by the master of objects such as a crystal, a mirror, or a peacock feather as symbols to help the student discover the nature of the inherent potentiality of their own state, and how that potentiality manifests as energy in various ways. Practice enables us to discover within ourselves the state of contemplation through which we find the presence of the master, together with the experience of the knowledge that he or she is transmitting.

In contemplation we find ourselves beyond the distracted state of our habitually confused minds, completely relaxed in the naked awareness that is our natural condition. In this natural condition, thoughts or emotions can arise, but they do not disturb us; we remain in the nondual state, integrated with whatever arises, without accepting or rejecting anything. Practicing in this way, we are able to remain in contemplation, working with whatever situation or circumstance we find ourselves in.

In the state of nondual contemplation there is really nothing to do or apply. There is no need to struggle with anything; everything can be left just as it is, with nothing to purify or transform. Then we discover for ourselves what is meant by The Great Perfection, or Total Perfection, which are both ways that the Tibetan word *dzogchen* can be translated. When we discover the self-perfected nature of our own state, we understand that Dzogchen is a word that, rather than referring to a tradition or school, really refers to our own inherent condition, the self-perfected state that is always there in each of us, but which is only experienced in contemplation. So contemplation is the most important of the Three Sacred Principles.

DEDICATION OF MERIT

The third Sacred Principle is the Dedication of Merit, which is a practice inseparably linked to our intention. When, for example, we do long-life practice, we do it because we want to have a long and prosperous life with as many positive factors influencing it as possible; but if that were to be our only intention, it would not be enough. We need to ask ourselves why we want a long life. We should not want to prolong our lives just in order to have more time for our business or for our political interests. We should do long-life practices because we wish to live for a long time in order to attain realization. If we live longer, we will have more time to practice, and if we are prosperous, we will have fewer obstacles to interfere with our realization. The purpose of realization is to benefit all sentient beings. This is why we are on the path.

We must be aware that the infinite sentient beings to whom we dedicate any merits arising from our good actions and practice have no knowledge of the teachings or of the path. This means that they experience infinite suffering. We are seeking realization not just for our own benefit, but with the awareness of the infinite suffering of the infinite beings in samsara. If we really develop this awareness, there arises a real, rather than an artificial, compassion.

The Buddha taught that we should observe ourselves, and that through observing our own condition there would arise the wish to benefit others. If, for example, we imagine ourselves in the place of those who are not on the path, we can understand how infinite their suffering is. Such beings have no guarantee of liberation, and that is very heavy.

Those of us who are on the path have made a connection through which we are not only able to receive and practice the teachings, but also, through the power of this connection, have a real guarantee that we will one day attain realization. We have the good fortune to have learned many methods, some of which, if we use them correctly, can even bring us to realization in this very lifetime. We must think not only of ourselves, but also remember the suffering of all sentient beings, and thus cultivate bodhichitta, the aspiration to arrive at realization for the benefit of all other beings. Applying bodhichitta in a way that is alive and concrete, we develop a real compassion that is not just a matter of words.

FALSE BODHICHITTA

Sometimes people speak a great deal about bodhichitta and love for others, but they never actually observe their own thoughts or intentions at all. Then everything they do can become a little like the games politicians play. Politicians promise all sorts of things, but often don't keep their promises once elected. For example, a certain party might continually make promises that if they are elected, they will provide everything the people need free of charge. But once they win the election they conveniently forget whatever they promised in order to get people to vote for them. Unfortunately, we sometimes do just the same, and claim to be practicing compassion for the benefit of all beings; but if we were to really observe ourselves and the way we actually behave in our lives, we would notice that in fact we never even relax our tensions enough to even get along with our own friends or with our Vajra sisters and brothers. We don't even have compassion for those close to us, let alone all sentient beings. This kind of falsehood clearly does not correspond to real bodhichitta, to the real expression of a pure intention to benefit others.

We accumulate merits through practice, particularly through the practice of contemplation. In fact, when we practice and find ourselves in the state of contemplation, we can accumulate infinite merits; and then again, when the teacher gives an explanation of the teachings and you try to understand this knowledge through your intention and collaboration with him or her in the field of transmission, you can accumulate infinite merits.

We should then dedicate these merits to all sentient beings. Once the merits have been dedicated, they always develop; they can never be destroyed. If you do not dedicate your merits and become distracted while losing your awareness, perhaps in the experience of a strong emotion such as anger, you can destroy in that one moment of anger the accumulation of thousands of kalpas of merits. That is what has been said by the great Master Shantideva in the *Bodhisattvacaryavatara*.[56]

Spelling of Tibetan Names and Words

Adzom Drugpa	a 'dzoms 'brug pa
Bardo	bar do
Bön	bon
Changchubsem	byang chub sems
Chetsün Senge Wangchug	lce btsun seng ge dbang phyug
Chöd	gcod
Chödpa	spyod pa
Chögyal Namkhai Norbu	chos rgyal nam mkha'i nor bu
Chörten	mchod rten
Dang	gdangs
Derge	sde dge
Dola Ser Shun	rdo la gser zhun
Dorje Sempa Namkha Che	rdo rje sems dpa' nam mkha' che
Drebunyi	'bras bu gnyis
Düdjom Lingpa	bdud 'joms gling pa
Dzogchen	rdzogs chen

Gar	sgar
Garab Dorje	dga' rab rdo rje
Gelugpa	dge lugs pa
Gompa	sgom pa
Gomrim	sgom rim
Gongter	dgongs gter
Guru Tsokye Dorje	gu ru mtsho skyes rdo rje
Gyalmo Tsawarong	rgyal mo tsha ba rong
Gyüd Lama	rgyud bla ma
Gyuwa	'gyu ba
Kagyüdpa	bka' brgyud pa
Kama	bka' ma
Kangyur	bka' 'gyur
Khandro Nyingthig	mkha' 'gro snying thig
Kunjed Gyalpo	kun byed rgyal po
Kuntuzangpo	kun tu bzang po
Kunzhi	kun gzhi
Lamnyi	lam gnyis
Lhungrub	lhun grub
Loden Chogsed	blo ldan mchog sred
Logpai kundzob	log pa'i kun rdzob
Longchen Nyingthig	klong chen snying thig
Longchen Rabjam Gyalpoi Gyüd	klong chen rab 'byams rgyal po'i rgyud
Longchenpa	klong chen pa
Longde	klong sde
Lü dultren	lus rdul phran

Lung	lung
Marigpa	ma rig pa
Milarepa	mi la ras pa
Naljor Namchö Mingyur Dorje	gnam chos mi 'gyur rdo rje
Namkhai Thadang Nyampai Gyüd	nam mkha'i mtha' dang mnyan pa'i rgyud
Nepa	gnas pa
Ngöndro	sngon 'gro
Ngöndzog Gyalpo	mngon rdzogs rgyal po
Nyamnyid	mnyam nyid
Nyang Tingdzin Zangpo	nyang ting 'dzin bzang po
Nyengyüd	snyan rgyud
Nyida Khajor	nyi zla kha sbyor
Nyimai Ödzer	nyi ma 'od zer
Nyingmapa	rnying ma pa
Nyingthig Yazhi	snying thig ya bzhi
Ogyen Tendzin	o rgyan bstan 'dzin
Pema Ledrel Tsalpad	ma las 'brel rtsal
Phowa chenpo	'pho ba chen po
Rangjung Dorje	rang 'byung rdo rje
Rigdzin	rig 'dzin
Rigpa	rig pa
Rolpa	rol pa
Rulog	ru log
Sakyapa	sa skya pa
Semde	sems sde
Semnyid	sems nyid

Senge Dradog	seng ge sgra sgrog
Shang Shung Nyengyüd	zhang zhung snyan brgyud
Shine	zhi gnas
Shitro	zhi khro
Sodogpa Lodrö Gyaltsen	sog bzlog pa blo gros rgyal mtshan
Tagnang	dag snang
Tagnang yeshe trawa	dag snang ye shes dra ba
Tampa Sum	dam pa gsum
Tawa	lta ba
Tengyur	bstan 'gyur
Terma	gter ma
Tertön	gter ston
Thalwa	thal ba
Thangka	thang ka
Thigle	thig le
Thödgal	thod rgal
Thugje	thugs rje
Tongra	stong ra
Tregchöd	khregs chod
Trisong Deutsen	khri srong lde'u btsan
Trulkhor	'phrul 'khor
Tsal	rtsal
Tsulshing	tshul shing
Tummo	gtum mo
Yangdag kundzob	yang dag kun rdzob
Yangti	yang ti
Yeshe migchig drima med	ye shes mig gcig dri ma med
Yidlhung	yid lhung
Yudra Nyingpo	g.yu sgra snying po

Zhi	gzhi
Zhichig	gzhi gcig

Notes

1. Tsegyalgar, Massachusetts, USA, September 1996. *The Mirror*, no. 38.

2. The first Dzogchen teacher of our era, who lived around the second century BCE.

3. The *Kangyur* (*bka' 'gyur*) is the collection of the original teachings of the Buddha. The *Tengyur* (*bstan 'gyur*) is the collection of commentaries. They were both translated from Sanskrit into Tibetan.

4. Bangkok, Thailand, July 1993. *The Mirror*, no. 24.

5. The three *yanas* are the three paths to enlightenment: Hinayana, Mahayana (both belonging to the Sutra tradition), and Vajrayana.

6. The Noble Truths of suffering, of its cause, of its cessation, and of the path leading to cessation. They are the foundation of all Buddhist traditions.

7. Oddiyana is the name of an ancient kingdom that many scholars have identified as the present-day Swat Valley in Pakistan. It was the homeland of Garab Dorje, Padmasambhava, and other Dzogchen and Vajrayana masters.

8. For a comprehensive study of the ancient traditions of Bön, see Namkhai Norbu, Drung, Deu and Bön: Narrations, Symbolic Languages and the Bön Tradition in Ancient Tibet (Dharamsala: Library of Tibetan Works and Archives, 1995).

9. Merigar, Italy, April 1993. *The Mirror*, no. 19.

10. The five aggregates, or *skandhas,* are form, feeling, perceptions, mental factors, and consciousness. Their purified aspect is personified by the five Sambhogakaya Buddhas, related to the five Buddha families: Buddha, Vajra, Ratna, Padma, and Karma.

11. A practice common to all Buddhist schools, often referred to as "calm abiding."

12. The peaceful, wrathful, and joyful manifestations are Tantric methods for transforming ignorance, anger, and attachment, respectively.

13. "Vajra brothers and sisters" is an expression meaning all those who are spiritually connected after having received Vajrayana teachings.

14. Merigar, Italy, July 1996. *The Mirror*, no. 37.

15. *Kun tu bzang po* in Tibetan, meaning "all-good."

16. Bois de Vincennes, Paris, France, July 1992. *The Mirror*, no. 20.

17. The Upadesha Series (*man ngag sde*), together with the Semde (the Series of the Nature of Mind) and Longde (the Series of Space), form the three Series of Dzogchen teachings. The Upadesha contains the highest and most secret teachings.

18. In Tibet there existed four main Buddhist traditions; the oldest, called Nyingma (whose adherents are called Nyingmapas), which arose in the eighth century, and three later traditions which arose starting from the eleventh century: Kagyüd, Sakya, and Gelug.

19. *Prajñaparamita* is a general name for a vast literature of Mahayana scriptures. The Madhyamika philosophy, whose main figure is Nagarjuna (who lived around the second century CE), is the pinnacle of the Mahayana philosophical tradition.

20. Mahamudra, or "total symbol," refers in this context to the highest teachings of the Anuttaratantras, usually practiced after having completed the process of Tantric transformation.

21. Kathmandu, Nepal, December 1993. *The Mirror*, nos. 26 and 27.

22. Another is Chittamatra, "Mind Only," one of the main Mahayana philosophical schools, founded by Asanga in the fourth century CE.

23. The six consciousnesses are the five sense consciousnesses and the mental consciousness. To these the Yogachara School adds the emotionally-defiled consciousness and the all-ground, or *alaya,* consciousness.

24. For a general study and translation of this tantra, see Chögyal Namkhai Norbu and Adriano Clemente, *The Supreme Source* (Ithaca, N.Y.: Snow Lion Publications, 1999).

25. *Rig pa'i khu byug,* with its commentary, probably by Vairochana, and *sBas pa'i rgum chung,* by Buddhagupta.

26. On this subject, see Gendün Chöphel, *An Ornament of the Thought of Nagarjuna: Clarifying the Core of Madhyamika,* transl. Pema Wangjié and Jean Mulligan; ed. Elías Capriles (Arcidosso: Shang Shung Edizioni, 2005).

27. The intermediate state between death and rebirth, which extends for approximately forty-nine days.

28. The Rainbow Body (*'ja' lus*) is the highest realization for a Dzogchen practitioner. At the time of death, the material body dissolves into the essence of the five elements as pure light, leaving no physical remains behind except for hair and nails. Many such cases have been witnessed, even in recent times. See Chögyal Namkhai Norbu, *The Crystal and the Way of Light* (Ithaca, N.Y.: Snow Lion Publications, 2000).

29. Moscow, Russia, May 1996. *The Mirror,* no. 36.

30. *Kun tu bzang po'i smon lam,* belonging to the cycle of the Northern Treasures (*byang gter*) called *dGongs pa zang thal,* discovered by the *tertön* Rigdzin Gödem Chen (*rGod ldem can,* 1337-1409). This text has been translated into Western languages. See *Five Dzogchen Invocations,* transl. Adriano Clemente (Arcidosso: Shang Shung Edizioni, 2005).

31. One of the five major texts received by Asanga, the founder of the Yogachara School; see n. 22.

32. *The Mirror,* no. 32.

33. Kathmandu, Nepal, January 1994. *The Mirror,* no. 29.

34. The four contemplations: calm state (*gnas pa*); nonmovement (*mi g.yo ba*); equality or nonduality (*mnyam nyid*); and self-perfection (*lhun grub*).

35. The term *khregs chod* has generally been translated as "breakthrough"

in Western publications, apparently on the basis of a different interpretation.

36. Namgyalgar, Australia, April 1997. *The Mirror*, nos. 40, 41, and 42.

37. According to the Dzogchen scriptures, Ngöndzog Gyalpo is one of the twelve primordial teachers. He preceded Buddha Shakyamuni, who is considered the last of the twelve. See Chögyal Namkhai Norbu and Adriano Clemente, *The Supreme Source* (Ithaca, N.Y.: Snow Lion Publications, 1999).

38. The description of these thirteen dimensions is mainly found in the *sGra thal 'gyur*, the main tantra of the Upadesha Series of Dzogchen.

39. See Mañjushrimitra, *Primordial Experience*, transl. Namkhai Norbu and Kennard Lipman (Boston: Shambhala, 2001).

40. Padmasambhava, also known as Guru Rinpoche, was invited to Tibet by King Trisong Deutsen in the eighth century CE. There he introduced both Tantric and Dzogchen teachings.

41. *Nam mkha'i mtha' dang mnyam pa'i rgyud.*

42. Some episodes of the life of Changchub Dorje (*Byang chub rdo rje*, 1826-1961) can be found in Chögyal Namkhai Norbu, *The Crystal and the Way of Light* (Ithaca, N.Y.: Snow Lion Publications, 2000). The biography of the female master Ayu Khandro (*A yu mkha' 'gro rdo rje dpal sgron*, 1838-1953) is included in Tsultrim Allione, *Women of Wisdom* (Ithaca, N.Y.: Snow Lion Publications, 2000).

43. *Nyams mgur*, the "experiential songs." Some of these songs have been translated by Adriano Clemente in Nyagla Pema Düddul, *Songs of Experience* (Arcidosso: Shang Shung Edizioni, 1997).

44. Chöd (*gcod*) is a system of practice that originated with the female master Machig Labdrön (*Ma gcig lab sgron*, 1055-1129). The principle of this practice, which combines the Sutra and Tantra teachings, is based on the "gift of the body" as a means to overcome attachment to the ego.

45. Adzom Drugpa (*A 'dzoms 'brug pa*, 1842-1924) was one of the greatest Dzogchen teachers of recent times.

46. The *Longchen Nyingthig* (*Klong chen snying thig*) is a very widespread cycle of teachings rediscovered by Jigmed Lingpa (*'Jigs med gling pa*, 1730-1792).

47. *Terma* (*gter ma*, literally "treasure") refers to teachings, ritual objects, statues, and so on which are considered to have been hidden by great masters and later rediscovered by special practitioners known as *tertöns* (*gter ston*).

48. Merigar, Italy, April 1993. *The Mirror*, no. 23.

49. Thödgal (*thod rgal*) and Yangti (*yang ti*) are special methods of practice belonging to the Upadesha Series of Dzogchen. They work on the principle of reintegration into the essence of the five elements. The Thödgal methods involve contemplation upon light, and the Yangti methods work with practice in the dark.

50. The Dance of the Vajra (*rdo rje'i gar*) is a special sacred dance whose movements are connected to the syllables of the Song of the Vajra (*rdo rje'i glu*), which is found in many Dzogchen Upadesha tantras.

51. The *Nyingthig Yazhi,* authored by Longchenpa, contains the highest and most essential Dzogchen Upadesha teachings in four series originally taught by Vimalamitra and Padmasambhava.

52. *Kama* (*bka' ma*) means a teaching whose transmission has never been interrupted.

53. New Delhi, India, November 1993. *The Mirror*, no. 28.

54. The translation of the original text plus a detailed commentary by Chögyal Namkhai Norbu are soon to be published under the title *Yantra Yoga: The Yoga of Movement* (Ithaca, N.Y.: Snow Lion Publications, forthcoming).

55. Tsegyalgar, Massachusetts, USA, October 1994. *The Mirror*, nos. 30 and 31.

56. Shantideva is one of the greatest Indian Mahayana teachers. He lived around the seventh century CE. His compendium of Mahayana practice, the *Bodhisattvacaryavatara,* or *Entrance into the Conduct of Bodhisattvas,* has been translated and published in various Western languages.